B2 Reading

Cambridge Masterclass

Simon Haines

© Prosperity Education Ltd. 2024

Registered offices: Sherlock Close, Cambridge
CB3 0HP, United Kingdom

First published 2024

ISBN: 978-1-915654-17-5

This publication is in copyright. Subject to statutory exception
and to the provisions of relevant collective licensing agreements,
no reproduction of any part may take place without the written
permission of Prosperity Education.

The moral right of the author has been asserted.

'Cambridge B2 First' and 'FCE' are brands
belonging to The Chancellor, Masters and Scholars of the
University of Cambridge and are not associated with
Prosperity Education or its products.

Designed by ORP Cambridge

For further information and resources, visit:
www.prosperityeducation.net

To infinity and beyond.

Contents

Introduction 5

Part 5 Multiple choice 13

Part 6 Gapped text 21

Part 7 Multiple matching 29

Practice tests 39

Answers 73

Simon Haines is an ELT writer, teacher and teacher trainer who has written a wide range of course books, skills materials and teacher handbooks. He is co-author of the coursebook *Landmark* (OUP) and exam titles *First Masterclass* (OUP), *IELTS Masterclass* (OUP) and *Complete Advanced* (CUP).

Introduction

Cambridge B2 First Reading

Welcome to this book on the Cambridge B2 First Reading paper. B2 First is one of the exams in the series provided by Cambridge Assessment – part of the University of Cambridge. It is the second in the range of tests they provide in General English:

A2	Key (KET)
B1	Preliminary (PET)
B2	First (FCE)
C1	Advanced (CAE)
C2	Proficiency (CPE)

The references next to each test refer to the CEFR Level (Common European Framework of Reference), and show the language level of each test. For CEFR B2 Reading, you will need to be able to:

- understand the structure and development of a text

- deal confidently with a variety of types of text

- understand the gist or general idea and purpose of a text

- understand specific information: main ideas and details

- understand the opinions and attitudes of the writer

- understand the tone of the text (tone can relate to the writer's mood or to the emotions they are trying to express)

- understand the implications of what you read (implications are ideas that are suggested but not stated directly)

- understand the links between various parts of a text, for example between sentences and paragraphs (this involves understanding words and phrases like these: *however, whereas, what's more, in other words*).

How does the test work?

You can take the B2 First exam on a computer or on paper. The content is the same for both forms of the test. The Reading section of the B2 First Reading and Use of English papers give you the opportunity to show your comprehension and reading ability with different types of text, such as fiction, newspapers and magazines, letters and emails. The B2 First Reading and Use of Engish paper consists of the following:

Time allowed	1 hour 15 minutes
Number of parts	7
Number of questions	Parts 1–4: Use of English (these parts focus on your knowledge of grammar and vocabulary) Parts 5–7: Reading • Part 5: six multiple-choice questions • Part 6: six gapped-text questions • Part 7: ten multiple-matching questions

There is more information to process in the Reading parts of this paper, so it is advisable to allow a little more than half the time for Parts 5–7.

Part 5: Multiple choice

This part of the B2 First Reading examination consists of a text followed by six multiple-choice questions. For each question there are four options: A, B, C or D. There are 2 marks for each correct answer. These questions check your ability to:

- read for detail

- recognise the tone of the text

- understand the attitude and opinions of the writer

- understand the main idea and purpose of the text

- understand the implications of what you read.

Part 6: Gapped text

This part of the examination consists of a single page of text with six numbered gaps. These gaps represent missing sentences. After the text, there are the six missing sentences and one extra sentence that does not fit into the text. These sentences are not in the right order according to the text. You have to read the text and the sentences to decide which sentence best fits each gap and which sentence is not needed. There are 2 marks for each correct answer. This part checks your ability to:

- understand the structure and development of a text

- make thematic connections between the missing sentences and the text

- recognise connecting words that link the text and the missing sentences (these may include pronouns, like *he* or *she*, determiners like *this* or *these*, or linking words like *however* or *therefore*)

- recognise key words in both the sentences before and after the gaps
- find linguistic evidence for your choice of answers.

Part 7: Multiple matching

This part of the examination consists of a series of questions followed by several short texts or a single longer text divided into paragraphs or sections. You have to match each question to a text or to the section of a text in which you can find the information. There is 1 mark for each correct answer. Part 7 checks your ability to:

- skim a text for gist or general understanding
- read or scan a text for specific information
- notice textual clues while you scan
- understand the opinion and attitude of the writer
- locate detail in a large amount of text quickly.

How to use this book

The main section of this book focuses on each Reading task type individually, explaining its characteristics and providing guidance on how to plan a response to an example question. There follow several exam-styled practice tests with detailed answer keys and commentary.

Each unit contains the following sections:

Prepare

This section introduces the question type, describes what you are are being tested on and gives you guidance and detailed suggestions to help you do well.

Practise

To prepare you for taking on an exam-styled text and questions, each unit contains a series of practice exercises with detailed answer keys that clarify how and why answers are correct. These exercises are shorter than the real exam, but follow the same format.

Put it to the test

Next there are two full-length exam-styled texts with questions. Again, there are detailed answer keys. You will find these keys especially helpful as they explain why the correct answers are correct as well as point out why you may have chosen incorrect answers (such as 'distractors').

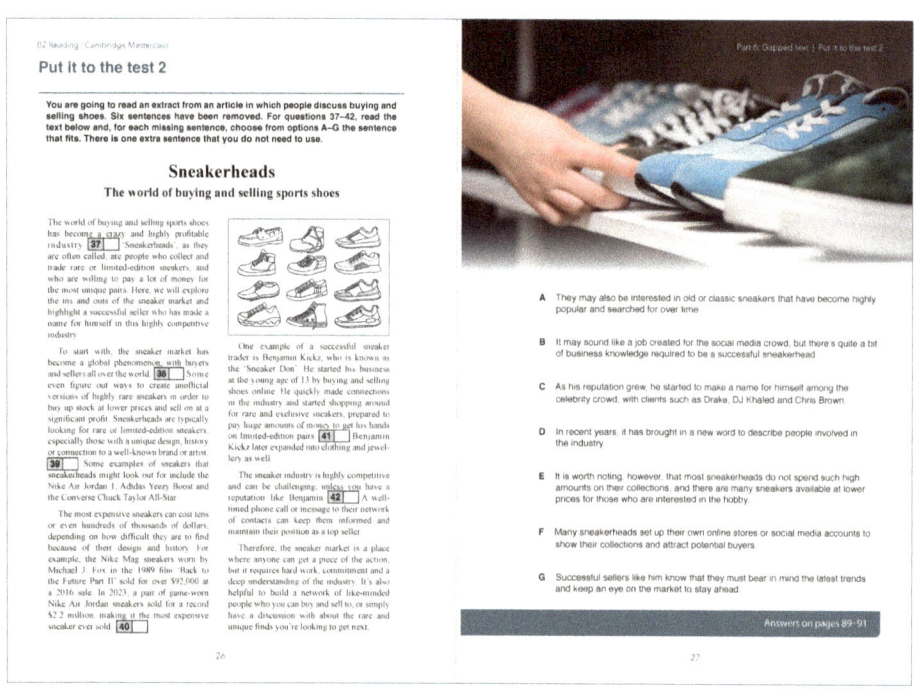

Answers

The answers to questions for each part are presented as follows:

Part 5

- The four questions are printed with the correct answer highlighted in a box.

- Below this, the part of the text and the four answers related to it (A, B, C and D) are reprinted, showing why the correct answer is correct and why the other three answers are wrong.

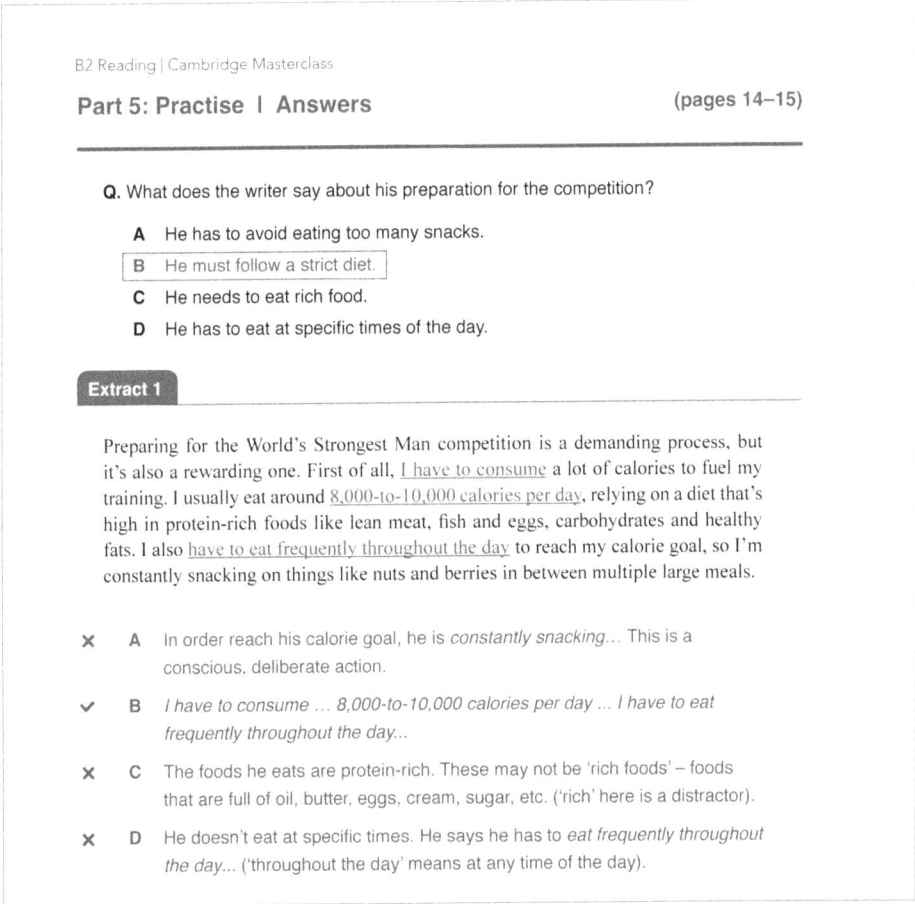

Part 6

- The full text is reprinted with the missing sentence included and highlighted.

- Words and phrases that link each missing sentence with the text are underlined in red. The links may be before and or after the missing sentence.

- In some cases the links are further explained by brief notes following the paragraphs. These are in red type.

- Occasionally the meaning of words and phrases is explained following paragraphs. These are presented in green type.

> Sneakerheads are typically looking for rare or limited-edition sneakers, especially those with a unique design, history or connection to a well-known brand or artist. **They may also be interested in old or classic sneakers that have become highly popular and searched for over time.** Some examples of sneakers that sneakerheads might look out for include the Nike Air Jordan 1, Adidas Yeezy Boost and the Converse Chuck Taylor All-Star.
>
> 39 A
>
> 'They' in the missing sentence refers to 'Sneakerheads' in the first part of the text.
> 'also' in 'also be interested' in the missing sentence is in addition to 'rare or limited-edition sneakers' in the text.

Part 7

- The ten questions are reprinted followed by the letter of the text (A, B, C etc.) it matches with.

- The words and phrases from the text that relate to the questions are reprinted here.

Part 7: Practise 1 | Answers   (pages 30–31)

1. Which person worked with teenagers?

   Text B: ...*camp was designed for curious minds* **between the ages of 12 and 15**...   **1 B**

2. Which person worked with children with scientific interests?

   Text B: ...*who were enthusiastic about* **science, technology, engineering**...   **2 B**

3. Which person mentions a weekly competition?

   Text A: ...*the sports* **tournament** *held at the end of* **each week**.   **3 A**
   ('tournament' = competition)

4. Which person tried to develop children's ability to solve problems?

   Text B: ...*encouraged critical thinking and* **problem-solving skills**...   **4 B**

5. Which person mentions that children's relatives saw what they had done?

   Text B: ...*demonstrated their individual projects to other children and* **their parents**.   **5 B**

6. Which person encouraged children to work together in groups?

Practice tests

The resource contains four B2 First Reading practice test (Parts 5–7) with answer keys.

It is important that you plan your time in the exam. You will need to finish all four Use of English parts to ensure that you leave yourself enough time for Parts 5–7. You should make sure that you:

- read the questions first, underlining key words and phrases

- read each question carefully and decide what information is needed.

If you can't find an answer quickly, go on to the next question and come back to it later. Importantly, remember that the text will contain **distractors** – pieces of information that may persuade you to choose the wrong answer.

Part 5: Multiple choice

B2 First Reading

Prepare

This part of the B2 First Reading examination consists of a text followed by six multiple-choice questions. For each question there are four options: A, B, C or D. There are 2 marks for each correct answer. These questions check your ability to:

- read for detail

- recognise the tone of the text (tone can relate to the writer's mood or to the emotions they are trying to make readers feel)

- understand the attitude and opinions of the writer

- understand the main idea and purpose of the text

- understand the implications of what you read (implications are ideas that are suggested but not stated directly).

Suggestions to help you do well in this task

- Read the whole text quickly before you begin the task. Don't stop to think about individual words you don't know at this stage. There isn't time to do this. The text may look very long but don't be put off; the important thing is to understand the basic meaning of the text at this stage.

- Read each question carefully and decide what information is needed. Look out for key words. Then go back to the part of the text where you think the information you need is. The questions are in the same order as the text, so the answer to Question 1 will be near to the beginning of the text and the answer to Question 6 will be near to the end. However, sometimes final questions may relate to the text as a whole.

- In the first instance, choose the option (A, B, C or D) that you think is correct. Check your answer by trying to rule out the other three options.

- Importantly, remember that the text will contain **distractors** – pieces of information that may lead you towards choosing the wrong answer. The way to avoid becoming distracted or 'tricked' is to read the questions and the text very carefully and find the exact information required by the question.

Have a go at some practice questions on the following pages.

Practise

You are going to read four extracts from an article about the World's Strongest Man Competition. For each question, choose the answer A, B, C or D that you think fits best according to the text.

Extract 1

Preparing for the World's Strongest Man Competition is a demanding process, but it's also a rewarding one. First of all, I have to consume a lot of calories to fuel my training. I usually eat around 8,000-to-10,000 calories per day, relying on a diet that's high in protein-rich foods like lean meat, fish and eggs, carbohydrates and healthy fats. I also have to eat frequently throughout the day to reach my calorie goal, so I'm constantly snacking on things like nuts and berries in between multiple large meals.

***

Q. What does the writer say about his preparation for the competition?

- **A** He has to avoid eating too many snacks.
- **B** He must follow a strict diet.
- **C** He needs to eat rich food.
- **D** He has to eat at specific times of the day.

Extract 2

Building up almost super-human strength requires intense weightlifting and functional fitness exercises. I train for several hours a day, six days a week, and I focus on exercises that will help me perform well in the competition.

It's important to take care of your body while training, and I make sure to warm up properly before each workout, stretch regularly and take it easy on the days when I'm feeling particularly tired or sore. At the same time, it's essential to push yourself to reach your goals.

***

Q. In these two paragraphs, the writer explains

- **A** that he never allows himself to relax while he is training.
- **B** that he concentrates solely on increasing his strength.
- **C** that his training exercises are always painful.
- **D** how he trains for the competition without damaging his body.

Part 5: Multiple choice | Practise

Extract 3

Preparation for the competition requires a great deal of dedication and sacrifice, and I've had to give up some of my social life and devote all of my time and energy to training. It can also be difficult to maintain relationships with friends and family who don't understand the time and dedication required to compete at this level. But I'm lucky: I have a network of people who understand and support my goals.

***

Q. What does the writer say about his personal relationships while he is training?

- **A** He spends no time with friends while he is training.
- **B** It's impossible for him to stay on good terms with people.
- **C** There is a group of people who are sympathetic to his aims.
- **D** He feels fortunate to have family support for what he is doing.

Extract 4

It also costs a fortune. There are gym memberships, supplements and equipment, as well as the high cost of travel from Iceland to many different competition venues and expensive accommodation for the competition. I mean, it's great to see the world while I'm competing, but it does come at a cost; I have given up a lot so I wouldn't miss out. But I have made up my mind to give my all to make it to the competition, and I believe it's worth it.

Of course, I couldn't do any of this without the support of my sponsors. It's vital to have a solid brand and a strong and constant social media presence. This allows you to showcase your achievements, training and personality to a wider audience and, for some competitors, attract potential sponsors.

***

Q. What does the writer say about the costs involved in entering competitions?

- **A** The main expense involved is travelling all over the world.
- **B** He doubts whether going in for this competition is good value for money.
- **C** He spends a lot on money on creating his profile on social media.
- **D** He is dependent on the financial support he gets from others.

Answers on pages 74–76

Put it to the test 1

You are going to read an extract from a blog post in which a professional gamer – someone who gets paid for playing video games – describes his work. For questions 31–36, read the text below and decide which answer fits best according to the text. For each question, mark the appropriate answer (A, B, C or D).

I remember when I first started playing computer games. It was back when I was just a kid, and my parents had gotten me a second-hand video games console for my birthday. I would rush home from school and spend hours on end playing games, as did a lot of children in my friend group, and I quickly became obsessed with them. My brother was the opposite and couldn't stand them. As I got older, I realised that gaming was more than just a hobby for me – it was a passion.

That's how I ended up gaming professionally. It wasn't an easy decision to make, and I thought long and hard about it, but I knew that I had the skills to compete at a high level. I have to admit that it took a lot of effort to persuade my parents to take it seriously, but their opinion meant more to me than any opinion of my friends. My father wasn't pleased when I told him my plan was to keep on playing games in my bedroom! I started competing in local tournaments, and as I gained more experience and success I decided to take my talents to the next level.

As a professional gamer, I earn money in various ways such as from winning tournament prizes, advertising money from streaming my games on websites such as Twitch or YouTube (plus online videos talking about the games) and even donations from fans. My dream would be for a big company to sponsor me, but that's a long way off. This industry is growing rapidly, and the potential for earning money as a professional gamer is increasing. However, it requires commitment, talent and hard work to succeed in this competitive field. And I'm 100% committed – I couldn't imagine doing anything else.

Nowadays, my days are a balancing act between practising, streaming my games to my audience, responding to comments from my followers and taking breaks to avoid getting too tired. When I get into my game setup in the morning, I fill out my schedule for the day – I might spend a few hours practising for the next competition, reviewing past games or taking part in online tournaments.

Despite how much I love gaming, there are times when I do get bored of it. Some people get addicted to video games, and it can be hard for them to step away from the screen. But when I feel that way, I know it's time to quit for a while and focus on something else. The cycling helps with this, but I also like to read or do some drawing.

The choice of which game to play can depend on various factors such as personal preference, skill level and the current popularity of a game. Some games can make professionals more money than others – financially, the big multi-player battle games are the ones to get into. As for my personal favourite, it's hard to choose just one. There are so many incredible games out there, each with their unique strengths and weaknesses. However, I have a particular love for League of Monsters and all the games that made me try competitive gaming.

Looking to the future, I have high hopes for my gaming career. I want to keep improving my skills, win more competitions and inspire others to follow their passions. The next step for me will be to get some sponsors, and I know that this will take a lot of hard work.

It takes a lot of nerve to pursue a career in gaming, but I know it will be worth it.

Part 5: Multiple choice | Put it to the test 1

31. How did the author get into gaming?

  A by playing a lot of games after school with his friends
  B by playing on a used gaming system he received
  C by playing online games with his parents
  D by playing online games with his brother

32. What does the author say about his decision to become a professional gamer?

  A He made the choice very quickly.
  B His parents fully supported him.
  C His friends helped him to make the choice.
  D It took him a long time to decide.

33. What does the author do to make money from gaming?

  A He has yet to make money.
  B He is sponsored by a major brand.
  C He relies on his fans to pay him.
  D He has several sources of income.

34. In line 21, what does 'my days are a balancing act' mean?

  A The author feels the pressure to perform for his fans.
  B The author has to manage many things simultaneously.
  C The author has days where he has to do competitions and promotion.
  D The author needs to manage gaming and another job.

35. In the fifth paragraph, the author talks about gaming and says that he

  A doesn't enjoy it as much as he used to.
  B thinks he will probably need to quit gaming soon.
  C usually enjoys it but sometimes it's not so much fun.
  D knows he has quite a heavy addiction to it.

36. Which games does the author say are his favourites?

  A The games that made him fall in love with gaming.
  B The competitive multi-player games.
  C The games that are the most popular at the time.
  D The games that can make him the most money.

Answers on pages 77–81

Put it to the test 2

You are going to read an extract from a blog post in which a health professional describes her job. For questions 31–36, read the text below and decide which answer fits best according to the text. For each question, mark the appropriate answer (A, B, C or D).

As a midwife, I have the honour of welcoming new life into the world on a daily basis. For those who may not know, a midwife is a health professional who specialises in supporting women when they are pregnant, as well as during and after childbirth.

Although I've always loved babies, I decided to go into this profession because I have always had a passion for helping others. After finishing high school, I considered going to medical college to become a doctor, but in the end I did a nursing degree. I then went on to specialise in midwifery, which I knew immediately was the right decision. It was the perfect fit for me because I wanted to work in a field where I could make a difference in people's lives, and being a midwife allows me to do just that.

It's not the best-paid job and my schedule depends on other people, but I wouldn't change it. The most amazing part of my job is being present for the birth of a baby.

There's nothing quite like the feeling of watching a new life enter the world, and I am honoured to be a part of that process. It's also incredibly satisfying to be able to provide support to new parents as they navigate the early days of parenthood.

Being a midwife, I love the relationships I build with my patients. It's not unusual for me to see the same women for several pregnancies, and it's always a joy to see how their families grow and change over time. Although I tend to be a bit hands-off after the birth, I still love being able to provide education and support to new mothers, and to see the confidence they gain as they become more comfortable in their roles as parents.

I've had the pleasure of attending a variety of births, from natural home births to hospital births with medical assistance. It's always a new experience to see the different ways women choose to give birth, and I've learned a lot from each experience. Last week alone I had one patient who was a professional athlete and continued running up until the day she gave birth, and another patient who came in to have one baby and left with twins!

However, in this line of work it's important to be able to think on your feet because things can change quickly during labour and delivery. It's crucial to be able to adapt to new situations as they come up. In the past, I've had to cancel birth plans and make quick decisions based on the safety of both mother and baby.

I remember one situation when I was attending a natural birth and the patient had turned down medication of any kind. Unfortunately, things started to change and, as the midwife, it was my responsibility to make a quick decision with the mother.

Even in those difficult moments, I know that I'm doing everything I can to give 100% to my patients. I realise that being a midwife is not for everyone, but for those who have a passion for it there's nothing else like it in the world. I feel incredibly lucky to be able to do what I do, and I know I will continue to find enjoyment in this career for as long as I do it. Despite how I feel, the job definitely has its challenges, like the emotions it produces in you and balancing work and personal life. For me, though, the rewards outweigh the challenges.

31. What led to the author becoming a midwife?
    A   She loved being around babies.
    B   She wanted to help other people.
    C   She worked as a doctor before specialising.
    D   She felt inspired by what she experienced at nursing school.

32. In the third paragraph, the author explains that the best part of her job is
    A   seeing a parent's reaction to their new baby.
    B   the salary she is paid
    C   the flexibility to work when she wants.
    D   being there when the baby arrives.

33. What does the author say about her relationships with her patients?
    A   She enjoys helping and informing new mothers.
    B   She usually only sees patients for their first child.
    C   She often sees new parents lose confidence.
    D   She is very involved in the weeks after the baby arrives.

34. By attending a variety of births, the author has been
    A   surprised that births often go more smoothly in a hospital setting.
    B   interested to find out that births usually require hospital involvement.
    C   surprised that births can be completely different for each person.
    D   interested to learn that births are different if the mother is a very active person.

35. In line 25, 'think on your feet' means
    A   to know how to deal with delivery issues safely.
    B   to carefully follow the birth plan.
    C   to be able to move around while working.
    D   to react as necessary at the time.

36. In the final paragraph, what does the author say about her career?
    A   She will be passionate about it for the remainder of her working life.
    B   She thinks the hardest thing is hiding her emotions from patients.
    C   She finds it difficult to give everything to her job, all of the time.
    D   She feels that everyone would enjoy the job if they knew what it involved.

Answers on pages 81–85

Part 6: Gapped text

B2 First Reading

Prepare

This part of the B2 First Reading examination consists of a single page of text with six numbered gaps. These gaps represent missing sentences. After the text, there are seven sentences that are not in the right order. You have to read the text and the sentences, and decide which sentence best fits each gap. You will not need to use one of these sentences. There are 2 marks for each correct answer. This part checks your ability to:

- understand the structure and development of a text
- make thematic connections between the missing sentences and the text
- recognise connecting words that link the text and the missing sentences (these may include pronouns, like *he* or *she*, determiners like *this* or *these*, or linking words like *however* or *therefore*)
- recognise key words in the sentences before and after the gaps
- find linguistic evidence for your choice of answers.

Suggestions to help you do well in this task

- Read the gapped text quickly to make sure that you have a general understanding of the subject. Then read the missing sentences. As you read these, underline any reference words, for example names, pronouns and times. These may help you make subject connections with the text.
- Don't choose your answers too quickly. First, try to match the subject of the missing sentence with the subject of the text. Don't forget that there may be distractors and misleading, incorrect connections. Remember, you do not need to use one of the sentences, even though you may think it fits into one of the gaps.
- When you have made a thematic link between the sentence and the text, check that the text and the sentence fit grammatically.
- Final check for sense: When you have finished the task, read through the whole text, adding in the missing sentences as you read. If you are not sure at this stage, look carefully at any answers you have doubts about to make sure that there are definite subject and language links between the text and the missing sentence.

Have a go at some practice questions on the following pages.

Practise

You are going to read two extracts from a newspaper article about the television programme 'Who Wants to Be a Millionaire?'. Three sentences have been removed from the extract. Choose from sentences A–D the one that best fits each gap (1–3). There is one extra sentence that you do not need to use.

Extract 1

The TV quiz programme 'Who Wants to Be a Millionaire?' is essentially a knowledge-based game show that tests the intelligence, quick thinking and bravery of its contestants. **1** Contestants must choose the correct option to continue in the game and eventually try to win the top prize.

One of the show's most famous features is the system of lifelines, which provide contestants with assistance when they encounter challenging questions. **2** The 'Ask the Audience' lifeline allows contestants to rely on the combined knowledge of the studio audience, and '50:50' removes two incorrect answers, leaving the contestant with a 50% chance of choosing the correct option. These lifelines add an element of strategy to the game, as contestants must decide when and how to use them effectively.

The success of 'Who Wants to Be a Millionaire?' is due not only to its engaging gameplay but also in the charm of its hosts. Throughout the show's history, there have been many different hosts, each bringing their own unique style and personality. From the popular original host, Chris Tarrant, who was presenter of the UK version for 15 years, to the current UK host Jeremy Clarkson, each host has left their mark on the show. **3**

The appeal of the huge prize has undoubtedly contributed to the show's appeal. Becoming a millionaire overnight is the dream of audiences around the world. The excitement builds as contestants progress through the questions, with each correct answer bringing them closer to the life-changing sum of money. The possibility of winning such a sum has made 'Who Wants to Be a Millionaire?' a fascinating experience for contestants and TV viewers alike.

A Their humour and ability to build excitement keep viewers on the edge of their seats, improving the overall experience of both TV and studio audiences.

B The first two of these are quite simple and are usually answered correctly by the contestants.

C The most well-known of these is 'Phone-a-Friend', which lets contestants call a chosen individual for help.

D This show consists of a series of multiple-choice questions of increasing difficulty, with a choice of four possible answers for each question.

Extract 2

An important factor that makes 'Who Wants to Be a Millionaire?' different is that is can be adapted to different cultures and languages. Including local celebrities and cultural references ensures that viewers will react to the show on a personal level. This strategy has contributed to the long life of the show as well as the global reach of the brand.

In addition to its television success, the show has expanded into other forms of media. **1** These adaptations provide an interactive experience in which players can test their knowledge and decision-making skills just like the show's contestants. The popularity of these games demonstrates the enduring appeal of 'Who Wants to Be a Millionaire?' beyond the television screen. Furthermore, the franchise's influence has even extended to the big screen with the world-famous film 'Slumdog Millionaire'. Directed by Danny Boyle, the movie tells the story of Jamal Malik, a young boy who appears on the Indian version of 'Who Wants to Be a Millionaire'. **2**

According to well-known psychologist Dr. Sarah Johnson, 'Who Wants to Be a Millionaire?' connects with our human brains in a way that makes it fascinating for both contestants and viewers. **3** This combination creates a powerful mixture of excitement and tension that causes the release of chemicals in the brain. The expectation of a potential million-pound prize stimulates the brain's reward system, making the experience highly enjoyable and turning viewers into addicts. This mix of intellectual challenge and decision-making keeps contestants on their toes and makes for absorbing television.

The worldwide impact of 'Who Wants to Be a Millionaire?' has been enormous. From its start as a television show, it has grown into a global sensation, fascinating audiences of all ages and backgrounds.

A She explains that the way the show works brings together elements of knowledge-testing, decision-making under pressure and the appeal of a life-changing reward.

B She manages to win the top prize by using her natural intelligence and ability to make quick decisions.

C It has inspired board games and computer games, allowing fans to experience the excitement of the competition themselves.

D The film explores the life experiences that help the youngster answer the quiz questions correctly.

Put it to the test 1

You are going to read an extract from a report that discusses the impact of Covid-19 on education. Six sentences have been removed. For questions 37–42, read the text below and, for each missing sentence, choose from options A–G the sentence that fits. There is one extra sentence that you do not need to use.

The impact of Covid-19 on education in the developing world

Online education isn't without its faults

The Covid-19 pandemic has had a huge impact on education worldwide, particularly in developing countries. **37** In this report, we will examine the impact of the pandemic on education in the developing world, with a focus on six specific countries.

At the beginning of the pandemic, many developing countries were forced to close schools and pause face-to-face learning.

38 Online education was not an option for many of these students due to a lack of internet access, computers and other necessary equipment.

In Nigeria, for example, a recent report by the United Nations Children's Fund (UNICEF) estimated that more than 10 million children are at risk of being left behind due to schools closing at the time. The report suggested that schools should have made alternative arrangements, such as radio or television broadcasts, to ensure that students did not fall behind in their studies.

39 According to a recent survey conducted by the National Education Association, 30% of Pakistani students did not attend online classes due to a lack of resources, while others struggled to keep up with the pace of online learning.

In Afghanistan the situation is even worse. Despite efforts in this country to build bridges between teachers and students through mobile phone-based learning, many students are still unable to access education due to a lack of devices and internet connectivity, as well as an unstable social and political situation.

40 In Bangladesh, for example, the government has provided free online education to students during the pandemic and has distributed radios and televisions to those who do not have internet access.

In Ethiopia, the government has also made suggestions to help students cope with the challenges of remote learning, including offering therapy services to students who are struggling to get over the mental health effects of the pandemic. Additionally, the government has been working with local organisations to provide students with books and other educational materials.

In Myanmar, where the pandemic has put the education of millions of children at risk, the government has been working to provide all students with access to online education. **41**

Despite these efforts, there is still much work to be done to ensure that students in developing countries are not left behind due to the pandemic. **42** They must also continue to explore alternative approaches to education and provide resources to help students get over the impact of the pandemic on their mental health and well-being.

So, while some countries have been able to adapt to online learning and provide alternative forms of education, others have struggled to keep up with the pace of change. Governments and organisations must continue to work together to find solutions to the challenges facing students in these countries, and ensure that they have the resources and support they need to continue their education.

A Similarly, in Pakistan, where many students rely on public schools, the pandemic put children's education at risk.

B It has been working with international organisations to provide devices and internet access to students who lack these resources.

C While some of these countries were able to adapt quickly to online learning and remote teaching, others were not so lucky, leaving many students struggling to keep up with their studies.

D With the help of these NGOs in the country, the government has managed to get a national news channel to broadcast educational programmes throughout the day, for different age groups and subjects.

E However, despite these challenges, many developing countries have been working to make up for lost time and to find ways to help students catch up with their studies.

F One major help would be for governments and organisations to take account of the unique challenges facing students in these countries and provide the necessary support to help them catch up with their studies.

G This was a huge problem for a significant number of students who were already struggling to get by on limited resources.

Answers on pages 88–89

Put it to the test 2

You are going to read an extract from an article in which people discuss buying and selling shoes. Six sentences have been removed. For questions 37–42, read the text below and, for each missing sentence, choose from options A–G the sentence that fits. There is one extra sentence that you do not need to use.

Sneakerheads
The world of buying and selling sports shoes

The world of buying and selling sports shoes has become a crazy and highly profitable industry. **37** ☐ 'Sneakerheads', as they are often called, are people who collect and trade rare or limited-edition sneakers, and who are willing to pay a lot of money for the most unique pairs. Here, we will explore the ins and outs of the sneaker market and highlight a successful seller who has made a name for himself in this highly competitive industry.

To start with, the sneaker market has become a global phenomenon, with buyers and sellers all over the world. **38** ☐ Some even figure out ways to create unofficial versions of highly rare sneakers in order to buy up stock at lower prices and sell on at a significant profit. Sneakerheads are typically looking for rare or limited-edition sneakers, especially those with a unique design, history or connection to a well-known brand or artist. **39** ☐ Some examples of sneakers that sneakerheads might look out for include the Nike Air Jordan 1, Adidas Yeezy Boost and the Converse Chuck Taylor All-Star.

The most expensive sneakers can cost tens or even hundreds of thousands of dollars, depending on how difficult they are to find because of their design and history. For example, the Nike Mag sneakers worn by Michael J. Fox in the 1989 film 'Back to the Future Part II' sold for over $92,000 at a 2016 sale. In 2023, a pair of game-worn Nike Air Jordan sneakers sold for a record $2.2 million, making it the most expensive sneaker ever sold. **40** ☐

One example of a successful sneaker trader is Benjamin Kickz, who is known as the 'Sneaker Don'. He started his business at the young age of 13 by buying and selling shoes online. He quickly made connections in the industry and started shopping around for rare and exclusive sneakers, prepared to pay huge amounts of money to get his hands on limited-edition pairs. **41** ☐ Benjamin Kickz later expanded into clothing and jewellery as well.

The sneaker industry is highly competitive and can be challenging, unless you have a reputation like Benjamin. **42** ☐ A well-timed phone call or message to their network of contacts can keep them informed and maintain their position as a top seller.

Therefore, the sneaker market is a place where anyone can get a piece of the action, but it requires hard work, commitment and a deep understanding of the industry. It's also helpful to build a network of like-minded people who you can buy and sell to, or simply have a discussion with about the rare and unique finds you're looking to get next.

Part 6: Gapped text | Put it to the test 2

A They may also be interested in old or classic sneakers that have become highly popular and searched for over time.

B It may sound like a job created for the social media crowd, but there's quite a bit of business knowledge required to be a successful sneakerhead.

C As his reputation grew, he started to make a name for himself among the celebrity crowd, with clients such as Drake, DJ Khaled and Chris Brown.

D In recent years, it has brought in a new word to describe people involved in the industry.

E It is worth noting, however, that most sneakerheads do not spend such high amounts on their collections, and there are many sneakers available at lower prices for those who are interested in the hobby.

F Many sneakerheads set up their own online stores or social media accounts to show their collections and attract potential buyers.

G Successful sellers like him know that they must bear in mind the latest trends and keep an eye on the market to stay ahead.

Answers on pages 89–91

Part 7: Multiple matching

B2 First Reading

Prepare

This part of the B2 First Reading examination consists of a series of questions followed by several short texts or a single text divided into paragraphs or sections. You have to match each question to a text or the section of a text in which you can find the information. There is 1 mark for each correct answer. Part 7 checks your ability to:

- skim a text for gist or general understanding
- read or scan a text for specific information
- notice textual clues while you scan
- understand the opinion and attitude of the writer
- locate detail in a large amount of text quickly.

Suggestions to help you do well in this task

- Read the questions first, underlining key words and phrases. Check that you understand what these words and phrases mean. The purpose of this is to focus on details you'll need when you read the text. At this point you could think of other words and phrases that have similar meanings. It may be useful to have done this by the time you go on to read the texts.

- Before you try to match the questions with the texts, read all the texts quickly for basic meaning. As you read, you may realise which paragraph or text matches a particular question. Make a note of this, but don't make a decision yet.

- Look through one paragraph or text at a time and read through all the questions to find the correct answer. As you do this, underline the part of the text that links with the question. This will help when you go back later to check your answers. Remember, there will be at least one answer for every text or paragraph, and there may be two or three.

- If you can't find an answer quickly, go on to the next question, and come back to it later. Don't spend too much time on one answer at this stage. This is the last part of the Reading examination and you do not want to be short of time.

Have a go at some practice questions on the following pages.

B2 Reading | Cambridge Masterclass

Practise 1

You are going to read two texts about people who have worked in summer camps. For questions 1–6, read the texts on page 31 and choose the correct text (A or B).

Which person:

1	worked with teenagers?
2	worked with children with scientific interests?
3	mentions a weekly competition?
4	tried to develop children's ability to solve problems?
5	mentions that children's relatives saw what they had done?
6	encouraged children to work together in groups?

Text A – Mark Thompson (Sports Camp)

I had the pleasure of working as a monitor at a Sports Camp last summer. The camp was full of energy and excitement, with enthusiastic campers aged 8 to 12 who were passionate about various sports. My role as a monitor involved organising and managing sports activities such as football, basketball, swimming and tennis.

It was inspiring to see the campers' determination to improve their skills and their eagerness to take part in friendly competition. We also included activities to build teams and create a sense of friendship among the campers. Through these activities, they learned important values such as working as a team, determination and how to play sports fairly. One of the highlights of the camp was the sports tournament held at the end of each week. Campers eagerly prepared for this event, practising their chosen sport and making plans with members of their team.

It was incredible to see their hard work pay off as they showed their abilities and celebrated each other's achievements. The Sports Camp was not only about sports; we also organised fun leisure activities to give campers a varied experience. From talent shows to treasure hunts, we encouraged their creativity and developed a sense of fun and community.

Text B – Emily Eastwood (STEM Camp)

Hi. My name is Emily, and I had an amazing time working as a teacher at a STEM Camp last summer. The camp was designed for curious minds between the ages of 12 and 15 who were enthusiastic about science, technology, engineering and maths.

At the STEM Camp, we tried to make learning fun and interactive. I had the pleasure of guiding the campers through a variety of hands-on experiments and projects. From building and programming robots to conducting chemistry experiments, every day was a new opportunity for the campers to explore and discover the wonders of STEM. One of the highlights of the camp was the science fair, where the campers demonstrated their individual projects to other children and their parents.

It was truly inspiring to see their creativity and determination. The atmosphere was full of excitement and curiosity as everyone exchanged ideas and learned from one another. As a teacher, my role extended beyond the classroom. I encouraged critical thinking and problem-solving skills in the campers by organising team challenges and group discussions. It was incredible to see their enthusiasm and watch them develop a deep passion for STEM subjects.

Answers on page 92

B2 Reading | Cambridge Masterclass

Practise 2

You are going to read two more texts about people who have worked in summer camps. For questions 1–6, read the texts on page 33 and choose the correct text (A or B).

Which person:

1. [ ] describes how the children felt proud of what they achieved?
2. [ ] mentions that children made something unusual for people to wear?
3. [ ] describes a camp situated in a wooded area?
4. [ ] describes activities that encouraged children to work together?
5. [ ] describes how the children became more confident due to their experience?
6. [ ] mentions that their group camped at night?

Text A – Lee Kass (Adventure Camp)

I worked as a teacher at an Adventure Camp last summer. The camp was located in the middle of a picturesque forest, surrounded by tall trees and clean lakes. Our campers were between 8 and 12 years old, and their enthusiasm for outdoor activities was catching! Each day at camp was filled with thrilling adventures. We went walking and rock climbing, and tried a variety of other sports. As a teacher, I was responsible for leading educational sessions that linked to the camp's activities. It was so rewarding to see the campers' curiosity and eagerness to learn. We explored the natural environment and conducted science experiments outdoors.

One of the most memorable experiences was the overnight camping trip. We set up tents near a sparkling river and spent the evening sharing stories and cooking food on the campfire. The sense of friendship among the campers was truly wonderful.

Overall, working as a teacher at the Adventure Camp was an incredible experience. Seeing the campers develop new skills and make lasting friendships was very rewarding. It was a summer filled with laughter, learning and unforgettable adventures.

Text B – Alex Rodriguez (Arts & Crafts Camp)

Hello, everyone! My name is Alex, and I had a wonderful time working at an Arts and Crafts Camp last summer. The camp was the perfect place for creative children between the ages of 6 and 10 who were passionate about expressing themselves through various artistic ways. At the Arts and Crafts Camp, we began exciting new artistic journeys every day. From painting and making sculptures to creating unique jewellery, the campers had the opportunity to explore their creativity and discover their artistic talents. As a teacher, I provided guidance and encouragement, helping the children to be imaginative and develop their artistic skills.

One of the highlights of the camp was the art exhibition, where the campers proudly displayed their creations to their families and friends. You could see the sense of achievement and pride that showed through their smiles as they explained the stories behind their artworks.

In addition to the creative activities, the Arts and Crafts Camp also encouraged personal growth. We organised storytelling sessions, where campers had the chance to share their own stories and take part in imaginative play. This allowed them to develop their communication skills and increase their confidence. We also organised art projects that required cooperation and the children to work in teams. Campers worked together to create large paintings and sculptures that created a sense of community and among them.

Put it to the test 1

You are going to read a newspaper article about volunteering for charity organisations. For questions 43–52, read the text below and, on page 35, choose the correct paragraph (A–D).

Give time, not money
Four people talk about supporting charities by volunteering

A. Kiran: Being a volunteer at the shelter – a place where people without a home can stay – has given me the chance to get together with, and get to know, people from all walks of life. We spend hours together, and I've formed some fantastic relationships with the visitors. I try to cheer them up, make them laugh and warm them up with kind words. It's amazing to see the change in them from when they first arrive, and it makes me feel like I'm making a difference. We don't just hand out food and go our separate ways. We have a bit of a laugh, talk about our lives and share our experiences. It's essential to treat everyone with kindness and respect, whatever their circumstances. Seeing the visitors smile and laugh, even for a moment, is incredibly rewarding. I'm grateful for the opportunity to volunteer at the shelter, and I hope to continue doing so for a long time to come.

B. Elisabeth: As a charity shop worker, I volunteer two afternoons per week to help out in any way I can. It's a great way to keep busy now that I'm retired, and I love being able to give back to the community in this way. When I'm at the shop, I spend my time organising and displaying items; helping customers shop around for the perfect thing. It's always interesting to see the variety of items that come into the shop that can now be sold for much less – from vintage clothing and unique home decoration to practical kitchen devices and children's toys. I suppose some customers buy items to do them up and then sell them on, but it's also exciting to find hidden gems that are perfect for my own home or wardrobe. Finally, I started volunteering to fill my time, but after that, I realised how practical and rewarding it is to be a part of this charity's mission.

C. Ivan: Taking a year out from university to come here to Syria and take part in volunteer work has been one of the most meaningful experiences of my life. Although there have been some very scary moments due to the conflict in the country, I know that I am making a difference and am helping those who have been affected by it. Every day, I work side-by-side with other volunteers and local aid workers to put up shelters, distribute food and supplies, and provide work training to those who have been affected by the conflict. It's humbling to see how much these simple acts of kindness can mean to those who are struggling to survive in such difficult circumstances. There have been moments when I have witnessed the courage of seriously ill patients or the commitment of brave colleagues, which reminds me to be grateful for the simple things I have in my life.

D. Carlos: Being a volunteer for The Samaritans is one of the best things I've ever done. I spend time answering the phone, ready to take calls from anyone who needs someone to talk to. The ability to listen patiently is key, and it's important to make sure that the caller feels heard and understood. Sometimes, all it takes is a kind word or someone to listen to help a person take back control of their life. Nowadays, with the world being so fast-moving and stressful, it's easy for people to feel lonely and that nobody understands what they're going through. By being sympathetic and listening, we can help make a difference in someone's life. It can be challenging at times, but I know that if I stick it out and keep doing what I'm doing, I can make a real impact on the people who call us in need.

Part 7: Multiple matching | Put it to the test 1

Which person:

43 ☐ mentions that they work somewhere that sells used items at a discount?

44 ☐ believes that helping those who have been affected by social or political violence is very satisfying?

45 ☐ describes how volunteering allows them to meet people from different backgrounds?

46 ☐ finds that volunteering is a great way to spend time now that they've finished work?

47 ☐ states that their listening skills are crucial for their volunteering work?

48 ☐ says that they're always curious about the range of things that end up at their charity shop?

49 ☐ suggests that the speed of modern life can make people feel alone?

50 ☐ thinks that they have learned to appreciate everything they have because of their volunteer work?

51 ☐ explains that they will return to their studies after their volunteer work?

52 ☐ says that it's important not to judge those that need help?

Answers on pages 93–94

Put it to the test 2

You are going to read a newspaper article about whether people prefer cats or dogs. Six sentences have been removed. For questions 43–52, read the text below and, on page 37, choose the correct paragraph (A–D).

Cats or dogs?
Four people talk about their pet preference

A. Laura: As someone who prefers cats to dogs, I've always found it annoying how dogs can be so needy. They're always wanting attention, and when they don't get it they'll bark and let you know. When I'm around dogs, I feel like I have to constantly run after them to make sure they're not getting into trouble or bothering other people. To me, dogs can do more harm than good, especially if they're not taught properly. On the other hand, I respect cats for their independence. They don't need constant attention or approval from their owners. They're content to curl up in a cosy spot and mind their own business. Sure, they may run away when they're not in the mood for socialising, but that's just part of their charm. Dogs, meanwhile, will do anything for a treat or to please their owners, but then they're right back to being needy again. For me, the choice is clear: cats are just better than dogs.

B. Marie: I always say: 'love me, love my dogs'. I can't imagine my life without them. They're my constant companions; always eager to back up my every move and wag their tail at the slightest sign of affection. I have a pack of dogs that I get along with so well – we go out together all the time. They're more than just animals to me – they're my family. One of the best things about having dogs is that they're the perfect excuse for a good walk. My dogs keep me fit and active, and I love exploring new trails and parks with them. Additionally, I absolutely love dressing them up in little costumes. It's enjoyable for me to see how nice they look and how much attention they get from people. But, at the end of the day, it's not about how my dogs *look*, it's about how they make me *feel*.

C. Carmen: On the one hand, I can appreciate that cats have their charms. But, they're just not as awesome as dogs. For me, cats are so arrogant. They'll sit on the arm of the sofa and look down at you like they're judging your every move. Dogs, on the other hand, just want to carry on and have fun with you. Secondly, let's talk about energy levels. Good luck trying to get a cat to fetch something or go for a run. Dogs will play until they get tired, and then they'll still want to go for a walk. They're well said to be man's best friend for a reason. And, let's not forget, dogs will do anything for a snack whereas I think a cat would eat *you* if they could. So, I would say the choice is pretty clear: dogs all the way!

D. Stephanie: I've been unsure about having a pet, but if I were to get one, I think I would go for a cat. I don't have any pets at the moment, but if I did I would almost definitely have a cat. They're independent creatures, and I don't think I have the energy for a dog. Plus, they're known to be cleaner than dogs, which is a definite plus for me. Of course, there are some things to consider before making the final decision. Cats can be quite independent and aren't so keen on affection, whereas dogs are known for their love and loyalty. However, I think I could live with that. Actually, the more I think about it, the more I'm convinced that a cat is the right choice for me. Now, the only thing left to do is to find the perfect one.

Which person:

43	explains that cats have bad attitudes?
44	thinks that it's nice when a cat doesn't demand affection?
45	mentions that they have several pets?
46	believes that despite the attention of strangers, their pets' appearance isn't important?
47	suggests that looking after a dog would take up more time than a cat?
48	states that cats demand much less attention than dogs?
49	sounds as though they're trying to justify the idea of getting a pet?
50	finds that training a pet is essential to avoid trouble?
51	believes that cats are less energetic than dogs?
52	explains that their pets help them to stay healthy?

Practice tests

Test 1 | p.41

Part 5: A Journey of Self-Discovery 42
Part 6: The Modern Face of Chess 44
Part 7: Earning a living as a musician 46

Test 2 | p.49

Part 5: Hay Fever 50
Part 6: Extreme Marathon Running 52
Part 7: Generation X versus Generation Z 54

Test 3 | p.57

Part 5: Tomato Growing 58
Part 6: The Joy of Bird Watching 60
Part 7: *The Parent* by Fabio Astrella 62

Test 4 | p.65

Part 5: Trends in Urban Planning 66
Part 6: The Rise and Evolution of Women's Football 68
Part 7: The Pitfalls of Wish Cycling 70

Cambridge B2 First Reading

Practice test 1

Part 5

You are going to read an extract from an article about making a journey on foot. For questions **31–36**, read the text below and decide which answer fits best according to the text. In the separate answer sheet, mark the appropriate answer (**A, B, C or D**).

A Journey of Self-Discovery

Deciding to take the challenge of walking El Camino de Santiago can be a life-changing experience for anyone. This ancient trail is a network of ways which lead to the cathedral of Santiago de Compostela in Galicia in Northwest Spain, where the remains of the apostle Saint James The Great are kept. Pilgrims, people who make the journey as an act of religious devotion, come from many different backgrounds and seek the transformative power of this famous path. Pope Alexander VI declared El Camino de Santiago one of the three great pilgrimages in Christendom. So, what are the motivations and experiences of the pilgrims who take on the challenge of walking El Camino de Santiago?

María, an enthusiastic traveller with a strong desire for adventure, wanted to connect with nature, find spiritual enlightenment, and test her physical and mental limits. The stories of self-discovery and the beauty of the path had fascinated her for years, and she finally felt ready to set off on the pilgrimage. "As soon as I began my journey," she says, "I quickly realised that the trail demanded my determination and ability to recover quickly. The hilly terrain, constantly sloping up and down along the path, tested my endurance, and the ever-changing weather required me to adapt."

María faced challenges like blisters on her feet, tired muscles and moments of exhaustion along the way. However, she discovered a strength within herself that she didn't know existed, pushing her beyond what she previously thought her limits were.

Despite the physical challenges, María found peace in the simple life on the trail. She says, "Each day was filled with walking on the ancient cobblestones, enjoying the stunning views of the Spanish countryside and forming connections with fellow pilgrims from around the world. People were an incredible variety of ages, nationalities and backgrounds, and everyone walking the trail seemed to feel a sense of shared purpose." María had serious conversations with these diverse individuals, gaining new perspectives and understanding of people on a deeper level.

The journey also provided María with time for self-reflection. She had moments to think about her life, her beliefs and her place in the world. "Walking the Camino allowed me to disconnect from the noise of daily life and focus on my inner thoughts and emotions. This introspection has helped me gain valuable insights into myself and my values."

One of the most enjoyable aspects of the pilgrimage for María was the breath-taking natural scenery. The beauty of the Spanish countryside, with its rolling hills, valleys and charming villages, left her in awe. Each new day brought fresh landscapes to explore and appreciate.

Now that it's over, María has taken some time to reflect on her trip. "Looking back on my journey, I realise that there are a few things that I might do differently if I were to organise it again. Firstly, I'd pay more attention to physical preparation, ensuring I was adequately fit and equipped for the long walks. Then I would plan the daily distances more carefully to avoid overdoing it. Finally, I'd spend more time interacting with the locals and immersing myself in the culture of the regions I passed through."

We mentioned earlier that walking El Camino de Santiago can be a transformative experience. María's motivations to seek nature, spirituality and personal challenges were definitely satisfied throughout her journey. But what were her thoughts after actually completing the Way?

Maria said: "I discovered an inner strength that showed me how much I could push myself to keep going. However, I had not considered how much my general fitness would benefit from doing such a physically demanding journey. I feel healthier physically, as well as spiritually." Maria also formed deep connections with fellow pilgrims. "I met people who I will always remember. I'm not sure I will ever meet them again, but I will always value the time we spent together. The simplicity of life on the trail allowed me to reflect on myself and appreciate the beauty of life. I will always keep my experiences in my memory and in my heart. It is an incredible experience I would recommend to anyone."

31 How does the writer describe the people who make this journey?

　A　They are all experienced walkers.

　B　They have the same motivation as each other.

　C　They have a variety of life experiences.

　D　They hope the journey will improve their lives.

32 How does Maria explain her decision to make this particular journey?

　A　She had heard other travellers' accounts of making the journey.

　B　She was determined to prove she was physically capable of walking that distance.

　C　She knew she would find the landscape along the route interesting.

　D　She had always been keen on adventures of this kind.

33 What did Maria appreciate most about taking part in this walk?

　A　The peaceful atmosphere along the route.

　B　Meeting people from many different countries.

　C　Meeting people who were very different from herself.

　D　Making meaningful contact with so many different people.

34 In paragraph 5, what does Maria mean by the phrase 'the noise of daily life'?

　A　The sounds associated with her normal home life.

　B　Everything she has to think about during her home life.

　C　The sounds that surround people living in towns and cities.

　D　Difficulties and challenges she has to face in her normal life.

35 If Maria repeated the experience, what would she do differently while on the walk?

　A　walk longer distances each day

　B　attend more events of cultural interest

　C　make more contact with people in the areas the route went through

　D　take more equipment with her

36 Looking back on her journey, what does Maria find surprising?

　A　That she made such good friendships with fellow travellers.

　B　That the walk had improved her physical condition.

　C　That life on the walk was so simple.

　D　That doing the walk would be so hard physically.

Part 6

You are going to read an article about the increasing popularity of chess. Six sentences have been removed from the article. Choose from sentences **A–G** the one that fits each gap (**37–43**). There is one sentence you do not need to use.

The Modern Face of Chess:
A Game Transformed by Technology and Popularity

Chess, often called 'the game of kings', has a rich history, originating in ancient India before developing and spreading to different countries where it gained popularity among the elite. Eventually it became popular throughout the world.

Throughout history, chess has been more than simply a game. **37** From the royal courts of medieval Europe to the coffeehouses of the 17th and 18th centuries, chess has entertained players and spectators alike. However, in recent years, chess has experienced a renaissance, capturing the attention of new generations and reaching never-before-seen levels of popularity. **38** This development has transformed the way chess is played and enjoyed. Online platforms and mobile applications have brought the game to the fingertips of millions, providing opportunities for players of all levels to compete. Platforms like chess.com and lichess.org offer a wide range of features, including virtual tournaments, interactive tutorials and the ability to connect with other players and fans from around the world. **39**

Moreover, technology has enabled the emergence of chess engines and artificial intelligence (AI) analysis, revolutionising the way players study and prepare for games. **40** These AI-powered tools have become valuable resources for both amateurs and professionals, pushing the limits of chess knowledge and enabling players to reach new heights of understanding.

Another significant reason behind the increasing popularisation of chess is the influence of television programmes and streaming platforms. **41** The Netflix mini-series 'The Queen's Gambit', with its fascinating storyline, has excited viewers and showcased the intellectual demands of the game. This series started a renewed interest in chess, and inspired a new wave of enthusiasts to start playing. Streaming platforms like YouTube have also played an important role in making chess accessible and entertaining for a broader audience. Grandmasters and skilled players now regularly livestream their matches, providing useful commentary and communicating with viewers. **42** The popularity of chess streamers has increased dramatically, drawing millions of viewers and making chess a spectator sport in its own right.

The combination of technology and media exposure has not only attracted new players to the game but has also expanded the player base. Chess, once considered an exclusive activity for intellectuals, is now accessible to anyone with an internet connection and a desire to learn. This inclusivity has allowed individuals of all ages and from all backgrounds to participate in the game and experience its unique challenges.

A In recent years, chess has found its way onto the small screen, captivating audiences with thrilling matches and colourful personalities.

B It has been a battleground for strategic minds, a symbol of intellectual ability and a test of quick thinking.

C Much of this new interest is due to the arrival of new technology and the rise of media platforms.

D The film was also a massive success with the majority of the critics who reviewed it.

E These platforms have created a global chess community, where players can learn from grandmasters, analyse games and participate in friendly competitions.

F This interactive feature has created a sense of community and camaraderie, with viewers participating in chat discussions and cheering for their favourite players.

G With powerful chess engines like Stockfish, players can analyse their moves, spot mistakes and explore alternative strategies.

Part 7

You are going to read about the lives of four professional musicians. For questions **43–52**, choose from the sections (**A–D**). The sections may be chosen more than once.

Which musician:

43	says they sometimes have to play at times they would rather spend with friends and family?
44	finds it difficult to make enough money from playing music?
45	enjoys playing with other musicians, but finds it limiting?
46	receives some of their income from audience members who appreciate their music?
47	plays music on celebratory occasions?
48	feels discouraged by the challenges they face?
49	says their pattern of work allows them time to get better at playing music?
50	finds it very difficult to find enough opportunities to play?
51	says they have no choice about what and how they play?
52	enjoys playing in a range of very different venues?

Earning a living as a musician

Four people talk about their profession

A. Being a musician is my passion: I eat, breathe and live music. However, the reality of trying to earn a living from music has been incredibly challenging. The journey of a struggling musician is filled with highs and lows, and I find myself constantly questioning my choices. Financially, it's been tough. There are few opportunities for gigs, and the competition is fierce. It feels like a never-ending battle to secure paying gigs, and even when I do, the compensation is often poor. It's depressing to put my heart into my music only to struggle to make ends meet. Emotionally, the constant uncertainty has an effect. I'm always experiencing self-doubt and I wonder if my talent will ever get noticed. But, despite these difficulties, there are still moments of pure joy. When I'm playing my music to a small audience that genuinely appreciates what I do, it's a real high.

B. As a guitarist playing in flamenco venues in Madrid, I've found a niche that allows me to earn a good living. It's an incredible feeling to have found success doing what I love. The 'tablaos' are bustling with tourists, and the demand for live music is always high. Financially, I'm finally stable. The tablaos pay well, and tips from enthusiastic tourists can be generous. It's rewarding to see my talent being appreciated and rewarded, allowing me to support myself comfortably. These shows provide a regular schedule that allows me to focus on my craft and continue improving. However, there are some negative things. Playing at the tablaos can be repetitive, doing the same thing night after night. Sometimes I feel my creativity is being limited. While the money is good, I miss the artistic freedom that comes with making my own music.

C. Being a musician in an orchestra has its perks, but also comes with frustrations that weigh heavily on my soul. I have a regular income, which is a rare thing in the music industry. However, the trade-off is a lack of creative freedom. Playing in an orchestra means sticking to strict musical interpretations and following a conductor's lead. While this provides a sense of playing together as a unit and discipline, it often feels like my artistic voice is not heard. I really want to explore my own musical ideas. Additionally, the repetitive nature of playing the same repertoire again and again can become monotonous. The excitement I once felt performing in a famous orchestra has become lessened. However, there are still moments I love. When the entire orchestra comes together, creating a captivating symphony, it's a wonderful experience. Those moments remind me why I originally fell in love with music.

D. Being a wedding singer is an absolute joy. It's an honour to be a part of people's special day and bring them happiness. I genuinely love my job, and I think it shows in my performances. Financially, wedding gigs provide a reliable source of income. There are many highs to being a wedding singer; witnessing the love and joy on the faces of the happy couple and their guests as I play for them is truly rewarding. Moreover, the variety of wedding themes and musical styles keeps my work exciting. From small garden ceremonies to receptions in massive houses or hotels, each event brings its own unique atmosphere and musical demands. Of course, there are also some lows. Performing at weddings means working on weekends and holidays, giving up personal time with my loved ones. It can be physically demanding, with long hours of rehearsals and different sets of music to perform.

Answer sheet

Part 5 *6 marks*

Mark the appropriate answer (A, B, C or D).

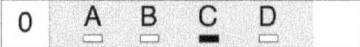

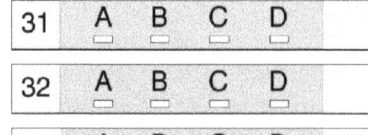
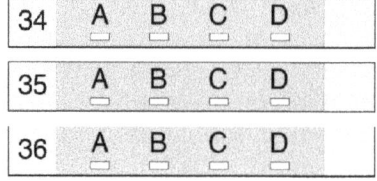

Part 6 *6 marks*

Add the appropriate answer (A–G).

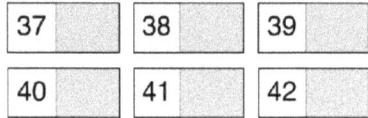

Part 7 *10 marks*

Add the appropriate answer (A, B, C or D).

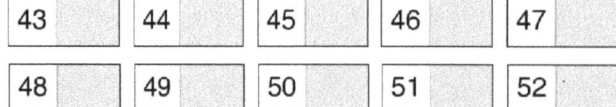

Cambridge B2 First Reading

Practice test 2

Part 5

You are going to read an article about a common complaint suffered by some people during summer months. For questions **31–36**, read the text below and decide which answer fits best according to the text. In the separate answer sheet, mark the appropriate answer (**A, B, C or D**).

Hay Fever

Hay fever, also known as allergic rhinitis, is a common problem that affects many people, especially during spring and summer. These allergies happen when our body reacts strongly to things it comes into contact with, such as pollen, dust mites or pet fur in the air. This can cause annoying symptoms like sneezing a lot, having a runny or stuffy nose, itchy eyes and an irritated throat.

Hay fever is increasingly common in many places, and there are a few reasons for this. One reason is the changing climate, which leads to longer pollen seasons. This means more pollen in the air, which makes hay fever worse. Another reason is that cities have fewer green spaces but more plants that cause allergies, such as ragweed (a plant that you've probably never noticed). Pollution in cities can also make hay fever worse. Additionally, changes in hygiene and less contact with certain germs, to which our bodies would have built up a natural defence in the past, might increase the chances of developing hay fever.

This annoying and often painful condition can really get in the way of enjoying life, but there are ways to manage it and feel better.

The main cause of hay fever is that our immune system, the body's natural defence to disease, over-reacts to harmless things around us. When we come into contact with allergens, our immune system releases substances called antibodies that make us feel awful. One common symptom is non-stop sneezing. It's like we can't control our sneezes and need to keep grabbing tissues to wipe our noses. It can be really distracting and make it hard to focus on work or studying.

Another annoying symptom is having a runny or blocked nose. It feels like we can't breathe properly because our nose gets swollen and makes a lot of mucus. Blowing our nose all the time becomes a regular thing. Sometimes, a blocked nose can even give us headaches and make our sinuses hurt.

Hay fever also makes our eyes feel itchy and watery. They can become red and sore, and can become super sensitive to light. It's hard to resist the need to rub them, but that usually makes things worse and could even cause eye infections. Wearing sunglasses or using special eye drops can help protect our eyes and make them feel better.

On top of all that, hay fever can give us a sore throat. It feels uncomfortable and makes us cough because our throat gets irritated by the allergens floating around. Talking or swallowing can become difficult when our throat is particularly sensitive.

Thankfully, there are ways to manage hay fever and make the symptoms more bearable. One thing that we can try to do is avoid the things that cause our allergies, but it's not always easy, especially when there's pollen in the air. Taking medicine such as antihistamine, which can be purchased without a doctor's prescription, can help by stopping the substances that make us feel bad. We can also use nasal sprays or eye drops to reduce inflammation and help us feel better.

If our hay fever is severe and doesn't get better with over-the-counter treatments, it's a good idea to see a doctor. They might give you a prescription for stronger medicines or suggest immunotherapy, which is a long-term treatment that helps our body become less sensitive to allergens.

In addition to medicine, there are practical things we can do to minimise our contact with allergens. Keeping windows closed, using air purifiers to clean the air and regularly cleaning our living spaces can help reduce allergens in the air. Wearing hats outside can also protect us from pollen. It's a good idea to check the pollen levels each day and plan our outdoor activities when they're lower. This information is sometimes included in weather forecasts.

Hay fever can be a real nuisance, but with the right treatment and self-care we can find relief from the symptoms. It's important to talk to a doctor to get proper advice. By taking steps to avoid allergens and using the right medicines, we can take control of our lives and still enjoy being outdoors, even when hay fever tries to spoil our fun.

31 How does climate change affect hay fever?

   A It makes the situation in towns and cities worse.
   B It leads to increased levels of pollution.
   C It affects the length of time when pollen levels are high.
   D It increases the number of germs in the atmosphere.

32 Why do hay fever sufferers react badly to things that should not cause them any harm?

   A Their bodies respond more strongly than they should.
   B Their bodies have a weakened defence system.
   C Their bodies have no natural defences.
   D Their bodies cannot produce substances that would protect them.

33 Why are hay fever sufferers advised to wear sunglasses?

   A Wearing sunglasses can prevent their eyes from watering.
   B Hay fever can make their eyes react more than normal to light.
   C Wearing sunglasses can prevent eye infections.
   D To prevent them from rubbing their eyes.

34 Why does the writer suggest hay fever sufferers try using sprays and drops?

   A They do not need to be prescribed by a doctor.
   B They can stop the allergic reaction to harmful substances.
   C They can stop sufferers from sneezing.
   D They can make their eyes and nose less painful.

35 Why might hay fever sufferers decide to see a doctor?

   A If they are particularly worried about their situation.
   B If their condition is not improved by medicines that can be bought easily.
   C If their condition is taking a long time to improve.
   D if they need to be treated over a longer period of time.

36 Why might hay fever sufferers pay attention to weather forecasts?

   A Some forecasts broadcast information about pollen levels.
   B To help them decide where to spend their time.
   C Because weather conditions can affect how hay fever sufferers feel.
   D To help them plan their day.

Part 6

You are going to read an article about a marathon runner. Six sentences have been removed from the article. Choose from sentences **A–G** the one that fits each gap (**37–43**). There is one sentence you do not need to use.

No Limits:
Journalist Simon Stone meets an Extreme Marathon Runner

John Davis is an extraordinary individual in the world of extreme marathon running. He has become a household name thanks to the reality TV show that followed him recently. Known for pushing his physical and mental limits, John has tackled some of the most challenging races on the planet. Let's explore his motivations and experiences and try to get a better understanding of this man.

"I've always been fascinated by pushing limits and discovering what lies beyond the limits of comfort," John explained when I asked him what got him started in Extreme Marathon running. **37** ☐ The thrill of completing that race started a desire within me to explore further."

Extreme marathons often involve running through difficult and dangerous terrains and enduring unpleasant conditions. I asked John what drives him to participate in those incredibly challenging races. **38** ☐ "I believe that by pushing myself to the edge, I can surprise myself by how strong I can be."

I asked John if he could share an example of an extreme marathon that left a lasting impression on him. **39** ☐ This was held in the deserts of Namibia where temperatures rose to more than 40 degrees Celsius. "The enormous sand dunes seemed never-ending, and dehydration became a real threat. **40** ☐ Crossing the finish line was an experience I'll remember forever."

The mental strength required for such races must be huge. **41** ☐ He replied: "Mental strength is undoubtedly crucial. When exhaustion sets in and doubt begins to enter my mind, I remind myself of the purpose behind my running. I visualise my loved ones cheering me on, and I draw strength from knowing that I am capable of overcoming any obstacle."

Extreme marathon running involves risks and potential injuries. I wanted to know how John reduces the risk of these dangers and ensures his safety. "Safety is the most important thing in extreme marathon running. **42** ☐ I also equip myself with the correct gear and supplies, such as a reliable GPS device, protective clothing and the necessary hydration and nutrition.

"To all those who dream of succeeding, I say: believe in yourself. Extreme marathon running is not just about the physical aspect; it's a mental and emotional journey. Be prepared to face difficulties, adapt to them and enjoy the victories, no matter how small they are. Remember, it's not always about winning but rather the personal growth you achieve along the way.

A He told me that one of the most memorable races he had participated in was the 'Desert Storm Ultra'.

B I asked John how he stayed motivated during the long and demanding hours on the course.

C John's amazing determination, mental strength and love for the challenge have taken him on incredible journeys.

D Apparently, It had all begun a few years earlier when he decided to challenge himself by running his first marathon.

E Before each race, I research the course, understand the potential dangers involved and do lots of physical training.

F However, the sense of community among the runners and a complete determination to overcome these dangers fuelled my spirit.

G "For me, extreme marathons are more than just physical challenges; they're a journey of self-discovery and personal growth," he said.

Part 7

You are going to read what four people say about modern generations. For questions **43–52**, choose from the sections (**A–D**). The sections may be chosen more than once.

Which person says:

43	Generation X has had to learn a lot about digital technology in a short time?
44	they lived through a time when the economy was unpredictable?
45	they were educated in a rather old-fashioned way?
46	their work depends on their ability to understand how shoppers think and act?
47	they appreciate having grown up in a technologically advanced world?
48	that members of the other generation are capable of doing many things simultaneously?
49	that Generation X is able to make links between digital technology and older ways of working?
50	that their generation understands the need to plan for the future?
51	the fact that their generation is both imaginative and technically capable makes them different?
52	Generation X has had to get used to the idea that business can be done digitally?

Generation X versus Generation Z
Four people talk about their generation

A. As a member of Generation X, I have witnessed huge technological changes in the field of education. Growing up, we had limited access to information compared to today's Generation Z. We relied on traditional teaching methods, developing critical thinking, face-to-face communication and an appreciation of books. Our ability to adapt to new technologies made us creative and adaptable learners. In comparison, Generation Z has grown up with a wealth of digital resources and instant access to information. As digital natives, they effortlessly navigate complex systems, displaying remarkable multi-tasking abilities and exceptional digital skills. However, despite their technological ability, I believe that our generation's advantage lies in our ability to solve problems creatively. Our experience of learning without the help of instant answers and our experience of diverse perspectives have created a unique skill set. We have a depth of knowledge that comes from processing and collecting information from various sources.

B. I belong to Generation Z, and am grateful for the technological developments that have shaped our lives. We are the generation known for our digital fluency, having grown up surrounded by technology. The world of digital tools, social media and online connectivity is our natural environment. By contrast, Generation X had to adapt to the rapid changes brought about by new technology. They possess valuable experience and a strong work ethic, but their learning curve for digital tools has been very steep. Our generation's intuitive understanding of technology gives us a natural advantage in fields that require innovation. With this strength, Generation Z brings a fresh perspective to industries that demand technological know-how. Our ability to adapt quickly to emerging trends gives us a strong position in today's tech-driven world. However, we recognise the strengths of Generation X with their valuable insights that bridge the gap between traditional methods and digital innovation.

C. I was born in 1975, so, as a member of Generation X working in the finance industry, I know the unique strengths we bring to the table. We grew up during a time of economic instability. Through our years of experience, we have developed a keen understanding of risk management, long-term planning and the importance of saving for the future. Generation Z, on the other hand, has grown up in a more financially inter-connected world. They are comfortable with digital financial tools and easily navigate online banking and investment platforms. Their fresh perspective and digital literacy are important in the fast-paced world of finance. However, our years of experience and deep understanding of financial systems give us a solid foundation to navigate uncertain economic landscapes. Generation X has lived through ups and downs in the market and economic downturns, which has enabled us to rely on our knowledge and experience to make informed decisions.

D. As a young person working in the marketing industry, I have a unique set of skills and perspectives. Our generation, Gen Z, has grown up in an era of social media and digital marketing, giving us a natural understanding of online platforms and consumer behaviour. We have perfected our skills in creating engaging content and persuading social media influencers to deliver precisely targeted marketing campaigns. Our ability to use creativity with technology equally well sets us apart. By contrast, Generation X has had to adapt to the rise of digital marketing. Their strengths lie in traditional strategies, which are valued by certain industries. However, our generation's ability to navigate the changing digital world and exploit the power of social media enables us to create innovative and visually attractive content that appeals to our peers. We have an ability to analyse social media trends and use emerging platforms to reach target audiences effectively.

Answer sheet

Part 5 — *6 marks*

Mark the appropriate answer (A, B, C or D).

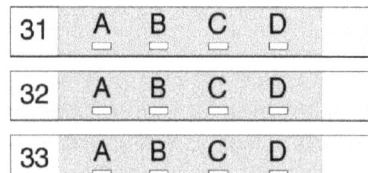
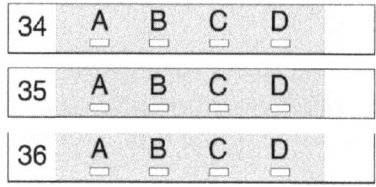

Part 6 — *6 marks*

Add the appropriate answer (A–G).

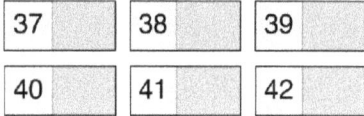

Part 7 — *10 marks*

Add the appropriate answer (A, B, C or D).

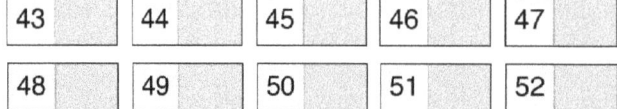

Cambridge B2 First Reading

Practice test 3

Part 5

You are going to read an article that gives advice about growing tomatoes. For questions **31–36**, read the text below and decide which answer fits best according to the text. In the separate answer sheet, mark the appropriate answer (**A, B, C or D**).

Tomato Growing

Growing tomatoes can be a beneficial and satisfying activity, whether you have an enormous garden, a cosy greenhouse or limited space. To help you grow tomatoes successfully, here's some valuable advice related to a variety of growing conditions.

Firstly, make sure that, right from planting your tomato seeds, you create a suitable environment. Tomatoes love warmth and sunlight, so place them in a location that receives plenty of natural light. If you're growing them indoors, think about using grow lights to supplement the natural light they receive. Keep them away from cold air and sudden temperature changes. Remember, a cosy, sunny spot will make your tomato plants feel at home.

Transferring your tomato seedlings into larger containers or the garden is a very important part of the process. Wait until the seedlings have developed a couple of sets of true leaves before transplanting them. Handle them gently, avoiding any damage to the delicate stems and roots. Remember, plants feel shock when they are transplanted, so be gentle and give your seedlings time to adjust to their new home.

For those lucky enough to have a garden, start by selecting the right location for your plants. Choose a spot that receives lots of sunlight and has soil where rainwater will not collect and drown your plants. If you plant them in a shady corner, they might disappoint you with a small crop due to the lack of light.

Prepare the soil by enriching it with compost – the decaying remains of other plants, or manure (the natural droppings of animals) – which will provide your tomato plants with the nutrients they need to become strong and healthy. Don't be afraid to get your hands dirty and dig deep. Remember, you get out what you put in, so invest your time in good soil preparation.

When being watered, tomatoes need a delicate balance; avoid drowning them with too much water or leaving them too dry. Water them deeply but not too often, allowing the soil to dry out slightly between waterings. Remember, it's better for them to be thirsty than to drown.

The main advantage of using a greenhouse is a significant extension of the tomato-growing season. In addition to this, the glass or plastic walls of a greenhouse protect plants from bad weather conditions. Ensure proper ventilation in the greenhouse to prevent your tomato plants from feeling like they're in a pressure cooker. Remember, fresh air is most important in a greenhouse.

Consider using wooden sticks to support your tomato plants and keep them from spreading all over the place like wild weeds. This will help the air to flow and prevent disease. Remember, a little support goes a long way.

Now, what if you have very limited space? Don't worry! Even with a small balcony or patio, you can still enjoy tomatoes grown at home. Select plants that will not grow large fruits because these are not suitable for container gardening. Get creative with hanging baskets, vertical gardens or even re-purposed containers.

In terms of caring for your tomato plants, regular pruning is essential. Cut off unnecessary leaves to help redirect energy towards fruit production. Don't let your plants go wild like a jungle or they'll become untidy. When it's time to harvest your tomatoes, pick them when they're ripe and bright in colour. Don't pick them prematurely or they'll taste sour. Remember, patience is important, and the wait will be worth it.

Now for the exciting part: preparing and enjoying your tomato crop. The possibilities are endless. Make some fresh tomato salads, roast them with herbs and olive oil or create delicious sauces and soups.

Growing tomatoes can be a very rewarding experience. Follow the advice above, nurture your plants like a caring gardener and watch as your tomatoes grow. Remember, with patience and care you'll soon be enjoying the delicious fruits of your labour.

Practice test 3

31 In paragraph 2, what does writer say gardeners should do to grow tomatoes successfully?

   A keep the temperature in the location cool
   B choose the best location and atmosphere for the plants
   C grow the plants indoors before putting them outside
   D make sure that the plants receive plenty of sunlight

32 What should gardeners remember when moving young plants?

   A Moving plants can damage their young leaves.
   B Young plants should be moved slowly.
   C Plants can react badly to being touched by people's hands.
   D Plants can find the process of being moved disturbing.

33 How should gardeners prepare their garden for their tomato plants?

   A They should add organic matter to the soil.
   B They should dig the ground thoroughly before moving plants.
   C They should replace their garden soil with new soil from a garden centre.
   D They should water the ground frequently.

34 Why would gardeners choose to grow their tomatoes in a greenhouse?

   A The temperature is warmer than growing plants outside.
   B The plants are protected from the weather.
   C Plants will produce tomatoes for a longer period of time.
   D The air in a greenhouse is fresher than outside.

35 What does the writer advise gardeners who do not have large growing areas?

   A To use containers on a patio or a balcony.
   B To choose plants that produce small tomatoes.
   C Not to use hanging baskets as they are unsuitable.
   D To find a way which suits their approach to gardening

36 Why does the writer advise gardeners to cut some leaves off their plants?

   A It helps the plants to produce a better crop of tomatoes.
   B Too many leaves make the growing area look messy.
   C Plants tend to grow more leaves than they need.
   D Fewer leaves on a plant make harvesting the fruit easier.

Part 6

You are going to read an article about a popular hobby. Six sentences have been removed from the article. Choose from sentences **A–G** the one that fits each gap (**37–43**). There is one sentence you do not need to use.

The Joy of Bird Watching

As the sun gently rises over the picturesque landscapes of the United Kingdom, a familiar song fills the air, signalling the start of a new day. **37** ⬚ There is a thrill that comes with being a bird-watching fan, a passion that first captured my interest as a small boy. Allow me to share with you this delightful hobby and say why I believe everyone should experience its charm.

Bird watching, or 'birding' as it is often called, is an activity that is bigger than just observation. **38** ⬚ For me, the attraction lies in the sense of connection it creates between humanity and the natural world. Through binoculars, we are given a look into another universe.

What truly sets bird watching apart is the deep sense of calm it creates. **39** ⬚ The simple act of walking through nature brings a much-needed rest from the chaos of daily life. With each step, worries are put aside and replaced by a sense of wonder as we encounter the avian treasures that live in these precious ecosystems.

Bird watching is said to develop a deep appreciation for the complex beauty of nature. The diversity of bird species that we find in our country is breathtaking, from the colourful feathers of the kingfisher to the majestic flight of birds of prey. **40** ⬚

As we become aware of the small differences in each species, we are shown the delicate balance of ecosystems and the importance of preserving them for future generations.

Perhaps the greatest gift bird watching gives us is the element of surprise. **41** ⬚ The excitement of spotting a rare bird, one that few others have seen, is an adrenaline rush like no other. This gives us a sense of achievement and adds to the desire to explore further.

While it may seem complicated at first, bird watching is an activity that can be enjoyed by all. **42** ⬚ All that is needed is an open heart and a sense of curiosity. The beauty of birding is that it can be done by anyone. Whether you live in a busy city or a rural village, there is always a world of birds waiting to be discovered right outside your door.

By becoming involved in bird watching, we open the doors to endless possibilities. It offers a new appreciation of the natural world and a deeper understanding of our place within it. We develop a strong sense of responsibility for looking after the natural world we see around us.

A   In a world with the constant background noise of technology, losing yourself in the beauty of the natural world can be truly therapeutic.

B   It is a journey into the heart of nature with an opportunity to witness the beauty of the avian world.

C   Every bird has unique characteristics, which demonstrate the extraordinary artistry of evolution.

D   Nature often presents us with unexpected encounters and rare sightings.

E   Bird watching is a hobby that allows us to slow down and take the time to look at the world around us.

F   It is the sound of our feathered friends, calling us to yet another wonderful bird-watching adventure.

G   It requires no special skills or extensive knowledge.

Part 7

You are going to read four reviews of a recently published novel. For questions **43–52**, choose from the sections (**A–D**). The sections may be chosen more than once.

Which reviewer:

43	thinks the writer was more interested in using words than with telling the story well?
44	says they found the pace of the novel was inconsistent?
45	believes the writer makes readers think about life today?
46	says that after reading the novel they discussed the ideas in it with people they knew?
47	found the story of the novel too pessimistic?
48	says that they found the novel interesting because of some surprising things that happened?
49	liked the basic idea of the novel but found how it was written as a novel disappointing?
50	didn't care about what happened to the characters?
51	praises how the writer describes the characters complete with their faults?
52	found the characters in the novel simple to connect with?

The Parent by Fabio Astrella

Four people review a new novel

A. *The Parent* by Fabio Astrella is a captivating novel that explores the complex elements of modern society. Astrella skillfully investigates human relationships, presenting an examination of moral dilemmas that really make the reader think. The story develops after a man slaps a child at a family gathering, revealing the hidden tensions and secrets within the group. Astrella's writing is honest and places the reader in the lives of diverse and imperfect characters. The story-telling is fast-paced, filled with powerful moments and some unexpected events that certainly kept me interested throughout. The author represents the various points of view and emotions of each character brilliantly, making them easy to relate to. Moreover, Astrella tackles important social issues such as parenting, cultural differences and conflicts between different generations with depth and sensitivity. *The Parent* challenges your own beliefs and encouraged me to have conversations about morality and justice with friends and members of my family.

B. *The Parent* by Fabio Astrella left me disappointed and frustrated. While the concept of the story seemed interesting, the way in which it was turned into a novel was poor in my view. The plot revolves around a man slapping a child; I found the characters to be unlikable and their actions often seemed to make no sense. The characters lacked depth and were often defined by their flaws and shortcomings, making it difficult to empathise with them. Furthermore, the way the story was told felt too negative and filled with unnecessary content that added little to the overall plot. Astrella's writing style, although raw and realistic, lacked sympathy and at times became rather unpleasant. I also found the development of the story moved too fast at times and too slowly at others. In summary, *The Parent* failed to deliver and left me unsatisfied.

C. *The Parent* was a disappointing read for me. While the novel attempted to explore complex themes and issues, I found it to be unnecessarily dark and without hope. Additionally, the manner in which the writer told the story from multiple points of view only added to the confusion and, for me at least, made the story feel disjointed. There were several potentially interesting characters, but I found it difficult to connect with any of them. Fabio Astrella's writing style is certainly gritty, but he often spends too long on explanations. For me, those parts seem more about the writer showing off his vocabulary rather than adding to the story. There was also an over-use of sensational descriptions of the more shocking content of the story. To summarise, *The Parent* left me feeling disconnected and disengaged from the story and its characters, and failed to deliver a satisfying and meaningful reading experience.

D. In Fabio Astrella's most recent novel, *The Parent*, readers are presented with an honest and thought-provoking representation of contemporary life. The author's ability to capture the most important characteristics of human nature and behaviour is remarkable, as he explores complex themes like family dynamics, cultural disagreements and the sometimes unexpected consequences of our actions. The characters are excellently described, each with their own strengths and weaknesses; their personal journeys can only be described as captivating. The story of the novel is told from multiple perspectives, a technique that offers a well-rounded view of events and allows readers to empathise with each character. Astrella's writing creates a strong emotional response in the reader and leaves a lasting impression. *The Parent* is a captivating novel that prompts readers to reflect on societal and cultural issues, as well as encouraging discussions about morality and justice in today's world.

Answer sheet

Part 5 *6 marks*

Mark the appropriate answer (A, B, C or D).

| 0 | A | B | **C** | D |

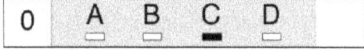
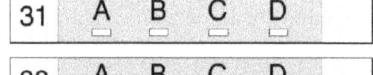

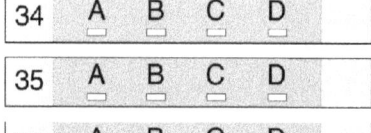

Part 6 *6 marks*

Add the appropriate answer (A–G).

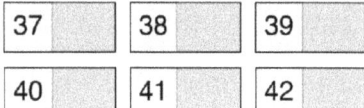

Part 7 *10 marks*

Add the appropriate answer (A, B, C or D).

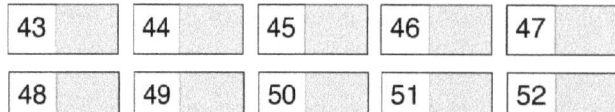

Cambridge B2 First Reading

Practice test 4

Part 5

You are going to read an article that summarises some of the issues involved in the planning of cities. For questions **31–36**, read the text below and decide which answer fits best according to the text. In the separate answer sheet, mark the appropriate answer (**A, B, C or D**).

Trends in Urban Planning

As the speed of urbanisation continues to increase, planners and policy-makers are increasingly considering new and inventive approaches to create more environmentally-friendly and long-lasting urban environments. Three important trends in urban planning have emerged in recent years: the concept of '15-minute cities', the adoption of green planning strategies and the rise of porous cities. These trends are revolutionising the way we design and experience urban spaces, with the aim of improving the quality of life for the residents while minimising the impact on the environment.

The idea of 15-minute cities has gained significant interest in the urban-planning conversation. The phrase, which was coined by Professor Carlos Moreno, emphasises the creation of self-sufficient neighbourhoods that can meet most of people's daily needs within a 15-minute walk or bike ride from their homes. In a 15-minute city, residents have easy access to essential amenities such as schools, healthcare facilities, grocery stores, parks and workplaces. By reducing the need to travel long distances to work and encouraging active modes of transportation, 15-minute cities aim to improve community cohesion, reduce traffic congestion and improve air quality.

Green planning is another key trend in urban development. With growing concerns about environmental decline caused by climate change, cities are increasingly prioritising strategies that minimise their ecological footprint. Green planning incorporates sustainable design principles into urban infrastructure, including the use of renewable energy sources, efficient waste-management systems and the preservation of green spaces. By considering and actively including nature into urban areas, such as 'urban forests', 'green roofs' and 'vertical gardens', cities can lessen the 'heat island' effect, improve biodiversity and improve air and water quality for residents.

Porous cities, or cities that prioritise permeable surfaces, represent a huge change in urban planning. Traditionally, urban landscapes have been dominated by impermeable materials, such as concrete and asphalt that restrict natural water drainage and contribute to problems, like flooding, due to too much rain. Porous cities, on the other hand, embrace the concept of water-sensitive urban design, where surfaces allow rainwater to filter through and be absorbed into the ground. This approach helps to replenish groundwater supplies, reduce flood risks and maintain urban areas in the face of climate change. Porous pavements, rain gardens and green corridors are some of the strategies used to create permeable urban spaces.

While each of these trends has different characteristics, they often cross over and complement each other in urban-planning strategies. For instance, 15-minute cities promote the ability to walk around in your town, which not only reduces carbon emissions but also contributes to healthier communities. Green planning ideas can become features of 15-minute cities by including green spaces, such as community gardens and pocket parks, within the designated neighbourhoods. In a similar way, porous cities benefit from both 15-minute cities and green planning by reducing the need for car-dependent travel and providing natural systems to carry excess water away.

Implementing these trends requires a multi-disciplinary approach and team-work between everyone involved, including urban planners, architects, engineers, policymakers and the community. It is crucial to get residents to take part in the planning process and to ensure that their diverse needs and points of view are considered. Moreover, effective communication and knowledge-sharing platforms are essential when passing on best practices in urban planning.

Cities around the world that have welcomed these trends and included them in their future planning have become leaders in sustainable urban development. For example, Paris has made significant progress in transforming itself into a 15-minute city by assessing and improving public transportation, creating pedestrian-friendly spaces and increasing the availability of essential services within each neighbourhood. Copenhagen, known for its commitment to cycling infrastructure, is also recognised for its green planning projects, including its extensive network of green spaces and efforts to fight climate change. Singapore has also emerged as a leader in porous-city design, with its innovative approach to urban water management, which includes extensive green roofs and the collection of rainwater.

31 What is the purpose of the current trends in urban planning?

    A to increase the pace of urbanisation

    B to reduce environmental damage done by cities

    C to make the lives of the people who live in cities better

    D to invent new ways of planning cities

32 What is the main attraction of 15-minute cities for residents?

    A Residents can reach the facilities they need easily and quickly.

    B 15-minutes cities help improve the quality of the air people breathe.

    C Schools and hospitals are near to where people live.

    D It takes only 15 minutes for people to travel from one side of the city to the other.

33 In paragraph 3, what is meant by the phrase 'ecological footprint'?

    A the amount of energy communities consume

    B the damage humans do to their communities

    C the amount of waste material communities have to dispose of

    D the impact communities have on the natural environment

34 From an urban planning point of view, what is the problem with concrete surfaces?

    A They are too common in many modern cities.

    B They do not allow water to run away.

    C They contribute to the effect of climate change.

    D They make it more difficult to establish 15-minute cities.

35 What is the main point being made in paragraph 7?

    A Planners should communicate with city residents.

    B Planning decisions should be made in a disciplined way.

    C Residents of cities should be involved in planning.

    D Engineers, planners and architects should all work together.

36 Why are three cities referred to in the final paragraph?

    A They are examples of positive urban planning.

    B They are examples of 15-minute cities.

    C They have improved transport systems.

    D They have introduced green planning policies.

Part 6

You are going to read an article about the growth in popularity of women's football. Six sentences have been removed from the article. Choose from sentences **A–G** the one that fits each gap (**37–43**). There is one sentence you do not need to use.

The Rise and Evolution of Women's Football

Women's football has experienced a remarkable transformation in recent years, changing from an under-represented sport to a global sensation that has captured the attention of millions. Here, we explore the progress made by women's football, highlighting its growing popularity, increased support and its impact on gender equality in sports.

The roots of women's football can be traced back to the late 19th century when the sport gained popularity among women in England. **37** It wasn't until the mid-20th century that women's football began to gain recognition, thanks to the determination of female players and supporters.

The breakthrough moment for women's football came in 1991 when the first Women's World Cup was held in China. **38** The tournament's success paved the way for future growth and investment in women's football.

Since the 1990s, women's football has experienced massive growth, with increasing investment from sponsors and attention from fans. National leagues have been established in many countries, offering professional contracts and creating ways for ambitious women to develop careers. The formation of the UEFA Women's Champions League further raised the status of club football, providing high-level competition and raising overall standards.

The rising popularity of women's football has also led to a rapid increase in participation from young players. **39** This has resulted in a larger pool of talent and a more competitive environment.

The visibility of female footballers has been crucial in inspiring young girls and challenging gender stereotypes. **40** Their achievements on the field, combined with their support for gender equality, have helped the growth of the sport.

Women's football has played a significant role in promoting gender equality in sports. **41** The increased visibility of women's football has contributed to broader conversations about equal pay, investment and opportunities for female athletes across all sports.

While women's football has taken tremendous steps forward, there are still challenges to overcome. **42** However, the progress made so far indicates a promising future.

Women's football has come a long way, evolving from a marginalised sport to a global phenomenon that continues to grip audiences worldwide. The increased support, participation and representation in the sport have not only increased the power of female athletes but also challenged traditional beliefs in society and advanced gender equality.

Practice test 4

A Gender pay gaps, inequalities in the amount of women's football broadcast on TV as well as limited investment in women's leagues remain areas that require attention.

B However, it faced opposition and was often criticised or banned due to negative social attitudes.

C It has provided the chance for women to showcase their athletic abilities, challenging assumptions about gender and sports.

D Organisations have been established to promote the sport among girls, encouraging them to take up football and providing opportunities for skill development.

E This will ensure that women's football eventually receives the recognition and support it deserves.

F Organisations have been established to promote the sport among girls, encouraging them to take up football and providing opportunities for skill development.

G This event marked a turning point in the sport's history, providing a platform for women's teams from around the world to demonstrate their skills on a global stage.

Part 7

You are going to read about one of the problems with recycling waste material. For questions **43–52**, choose from the sections (**A–D**). The sections may be chosen more than once.

Which paragraph:

43	suggests that makers should be responsible for the whole life of their products?
44	points out that recycling companies may lose business if the incorrect goods are mixed in with recyclable items?
45	includes lists of materials that could replace plastic packaging?
46	explains that a mixture of recyclable and unrecyclable goods may end up being buried in the ground?
47	suggests that consumers should find out for themselves the recycling policies in their area?
48	points out that different regions may have different recycling policies?
49	includes a list of materials that some consumers put in recycling bins even if they are not sure they can be recycled?
50	says consumers should no longer depend on products that can only be used once?
51	suggests that makers state clearly whether their products can be recycled?
52	suggests that new laws could be brought in to improve the situation?

The Pitfalls of Wish Cycling: A Vicious Cycle of Waste

Four people talk about recycling waste material

A. In the interests of protecting the environment, it is essential to adopt responsible waste-management practices. However, despite good intentions, some individuals contribute to 'wish cycling', which often has unwanted consequences and impedes recycling efforts. Wish cycling comes from a genuine desire to do the right thing for the environment. It occurs when individuals, unsure if an item can be recycled, place it in the recycling bin hoping that it will be properly sorted and recycled. Common examples include plastic bags, polystyrene foam and certain plastics that may or may not be accepted by recycling facilities. Unfortunately, wish cycling can have negative effects on the entire recycling process. One of the major resulting problems is contamination. When non-recyclable items are mixed with recyclables, they make sorting and processing material very difficult. Contamination lowers the quality of recycled materials and can make entire batches impossible to recycle. Consequently, recycling facilities have to send contaminated materials to waste landfill sites, negating the efforts of responsible recyclers.

B. A widespread lack of understanding of recycling instructions and rules contributes to wish cycling. Many individuals are unsure about what can and cannot be recycled, something that creates the mistaken belief that any item with a recycling symbol can be placed in the recycling bin. This knowledge gap highlights the need for improved education on recycling practices, including clear and accessible information regarding local recycling programmes that differ widely from area to area. When non-recyclable items are mistakenly placed in recycling bins, recycling facilities struggle to manage the materials that have been wrongly sorted. Consequently, recycling processes become less efficient, and the overall quality of recycled materials decreases. As a result, recycling companies face challenges in marketing their products, and this leads to decreased demand for recycled goods.

C. To fight against wish cycling and its negative consequences, it is necessary for us to develop an approach that considers many different factors. Firstly, and most importantly, individuals must inform themselves about local recycling services and guidelines. Education has a part to play here. Governments and recycling organisations have a vital role to play in this process by providing clear and accessible information, including online resources and recycling guides, to help people make informed decisions. Additionally, reducing waste at the source through conscious consumption behaviour is crucial. Shoppers should be persuaded to choose alternatives to plastic packaging that can be reused; alternatives such as cloth bags, goods sold in carboard packages, refillable water bottles and other containers. Individual consumers can significantly reduce the extent to which they rely on single-use items. This would have the effect of minimising the need for recycling altogether.

D. Efforts by manufacturers, policymakers and waste-management organisations are essential if recycling is to be effective. Manufacturers can play a vital role by developing more sustainable packaging solutions by reducing the use of non-recyclable materials and by clearly labelling products to inform consumers about recyclability. Policymakers in governments can introduce legislation to encourage manufacturers to take responsibility for the entire life-cycle of their products. Wish cycling, although well-intentioned, presents significant challenges to effective waste management and recycling. Contamination, increased costs and a shrinking market for recycled goods are among the negative results of wish cycling. By concentrating on education, persuading consumers to be aware of their behaviour consumption and encouraging all those involved to collaborate, we can break wish cycling behaviour and create a more sustainable future.

Answer sheet

Part 5 *6 marks*

Mark the appropriate answer (A, B, C or D).

| 0 | A ☐ B ☐ C ■ D ☐ |

31	A ☐ B ☐ C ☐ D ☐		34	A ☐ B ☐ C ☐ D ☐
32	A ☐ B ☐ C ☐ D ☐		35	A ☐ B ☐ C ☐ D ☐
33	A ☐ B ☐ C ☐ D ☐		36	A ☐ B ☐ C ☐ D ☐

Part 6 *6 marks*

Add the appropriate answer (A–G).

| 37 | 38 | 39 |
| 40 | 41 | 42 |

Part 7 *10 marks*

Add the appropriate answer (A, B, C or D).

| 43 | 44 | 45 | 46 | 47 |
| 48 | 49 | 50 | 51 | 52 |

Answers

Part 5: Multiple choice | p.74

Practise 74
Put it to the test 1 77
Put it to the test 2 81

Part 6: Gapped text | p.86

Practise 86
Put it to the test 1 88
Put it to the test 2 89

Part 7: Multiple matching | p.92

Practise 1 92
Practise 2 92
Put it to the test 1 93
Put it to the test 2 94

Practice tests | p.96

Test 1 96
Test 2 98
Test 3 100
Test 4 102

B2 Reading | Cambridge Masterclass

Part 5: Practise | Answers (pages 14–15)

Q. What does the writer say about his preparation for the competition?

- A He has to avoid eating too many snacks.
- B He must follow a strict diet.
- C He needs to eat rich food.
- D He has to eat at specific times of the day.

Extract 1

Preparing for the World's Strongest Man competition is a demanding process, but it's also a rewarding one. First of all, <u>I have to consume</u> a lot of calories to fuel my training. I usually eat around <u>8,000-to-10,000 calories per day</u>, relying on a diet that's high in protein-rich foods like lean meat, fish and eggs, carbohydrates and healthy fats. I also <u>have to eat frequently throughout the day</u> to reach my calorie goal, so I'm constantly snacking on things like nuts and berries in between multiple large meals.

✗ A In order reach his calorie goal, he is *constantly snacking...* This is a conscious, deliberate action.

✓ B *I have to consume ... 8,000-to-10,000 calories per day ... I have to eat frequently throughout the day...*

✗ C The foods he eats are protein-rich. These may not be 'rich foods' – foods that are full of oil, butter, eggs, cream, sugar, etc. ('rich' here is a distractor).

✗ D He doesn't eat at specific times. He says he has to *eat frequently throughout the day...* ('throughout the day' means at any time of the day).

Q. In these two paragraphs, the writer explains

- A that he never allows himself to relax while he is training.
- B that he concentrates solely on increasing his strength.
- C that his training exercises are always painful.
- D how he trains for the competition without damaging his body.

Watch out for distractors — information that may lead to choosing a wrong answer!

74

Answers | Part 5

Extract 2

Building up almost super-human strength requires intense weightlifting and functional fitness exercises. I train for several hours a day, six days a week, and I focus on exercises that will help me perform well in the competition.

<u>It's important to take care of your body while training</u>, and I make sure to warm up properly before each workout, stretch regularly and take it easy on the days when I'm feeling particularly tired or sore. At the same time, it's essential to push yourself to reach your goals.

✗   A   He allows himself to relax if he feels he is damaging his health: *take it easy on the days when I'm feeling particularly tired or sore*. The word 'never' makes this answer incorrect.

✗   B   As well as increasing his strength by weightlifting, he does *functional fitness exercises* and *exercises that will help me perform well in the competition*. The word 'solely' is the reason that this answer is not correct.

✗   C   The word 'always' makes this answer incorrect. The writer refers to *days when I'm feeling particularly tired or sore*. This means that there are some days when he does not feel tired or sore.

✓   D   The first paragraph describes what he has to do to train physically. The second paragraph explains how he looks after his body at the same time as training effectively.

Q. What does the writer say about his personal relationships while he is training?

A   He spends no time with friends while he is training.
B   It's impossible for him to stay on good terms with people.
C   There is a group of people who are sympathetic to his aims.
D   He feels fortunate to have family support for what he is doing.

Extract 3

Preparation for the competition requires a great deal of dedication and sacrifice, and I've had to give up some of my social life and devote all of my time and energy to training. It can also be difficult to maintain relationships with friends and family who don't understand the time and dedication required to compete at this level. But I'm lucky: <u>I have a network of people who understand and support my goals</u>.

✗	A	The writer says he has *had to give up some of my social life* – not all of it.
✗	B	It is not 'impossible'; *it's difficult to maintain relationships*. The phrase *to stay on good terms with* is more negative than *maintain relationships*.
✓	C	He says he has *a network of people who understand and support my goals*.
✗	D	The *network of people* he refers to is not restricted to family members.

Q. What does the writer say about the costs involved in entering competitions?

- A The main expense involved is travelling all over the world.
- B He doubts whether going in for this competition is good value for money.
- C He spends a lot on money on creating his profile on social media.
- D He is dependent on the financial support he gets from others.

Extract 4

It also costs a fortune. There are gym memberships, supplements and equipment, as well as the high cost of travel from Iceland to many different competition venues and expensive lodging for the competition. I mean, it's great to see the world while I'm competing, but it does come at a cost; I have given up a lot so I wouldn't miss out. But I have made up my mind to give my all to make it to the competition, and I believe it's worth it.

Of course, I couldn't do any of this without the support of my sponsors. It's vital to have a solid brand and a strong and constant social media presence. This allows you to showcase your achievements, training and personality to a wider audience and, for some competitors, attract potential sponsors.

✗	A	*The high cost of travel from Iceland to many different competition venues* is listed as one of the expenses involved but not the main one.
✗	B	Having listed the expense of competing, he says *I believe it's worth it*. The expression 'worth it' can also be a reference to other things he has had to give up to continue competing. The word 'value' is a distractor.
✗	C	He stresses the importance of *a strong and constant social media presence* but does not mention whether this is a financial expense.
✓	D	Having listed how expensive going in for competitions is, the writer says *I couldn't do any of this without the support of my sponsors*.

Part 5: Put it to the test 1 | Answers (pages 16–17)

31. How did the author get into gaming?

- A by playing a lot of games after school with his friends
- **B by playing on a used gaming system he received**
- C by playing online games with his parents
- D by playing online games with his brother

Paragraph 1

I remember when I first started playing computer games. It was back when I was just a kid, and my parents had gotten me a second-hand video games console for my birthday. I would rush home from school and spend hours on end playing games, as did a lot of children in my friend group, and I quickly became obsessed with them. My brother was the opposite and couldn't stand them. As I got older, I realised that gaming was more than just a hobby for me – it was a passion.

✗ A He played in his bedroom. The only mention of 'friends' is *as did a lot of children in my friend group...* They did the same as he did: they played alone.

✓ B 'used gaming system he received' – *my parents had gotten me a second-hand video games console...* This was a birthday gift ('used' = second hand).

✗ C His parents are mentioned but only because they gave him the system.

✗ D His brother was his opposite: *My brother... couldn't stand them* ('them' = the games).

Remember: In the first instance, choose the option (A, B, C or D) that you think is correct. Check your answer by trying to rule out the other three options.

---

32. What does the author say about his decision to become a professional gamer?

- A He made the choice very quickly.
- B His parents fully supported him.
- C His friends helped him to make the choice.
- **D It took him a long time to decide.**

Paragraph 2

That's how I ended up gaming professionally. <u>It wasn't an easy decision to make, and I thought long and hard about it</u>, but I knew that I had the skills to compete at a high level. I have to admit that it took a lot of effort to persuade my parents to take it seriously, but their opinion meant more to me than any opinion of my friends. My father wasn't pleased when I told him my plan was to keep on playing games in my bedroom! I started competing in local tournaments, and, as I gained more experience and success I decided to take my talents to the next level.

✗ **A** He did not make the choice quickly — he *thought long and hard about it.*

✗ **B** His parents didn't support him fully — *it took a lot of me persuading my parents to take it seriously / My father wasn't pleased.*

✗ **C** He refers to friends but only to say that their opinion was less important than his parents' opinion.

✓ **D** 'the decision to become a professional gamer' — *It wasn't an easy decision to make, and I thought long and hard about it.*

---

33. What does the author do to make money from gaming?

    A He has yet to make money.

    B He is sponsored by a major brand.

    C He relies on his fans to pay him.

    D He has several sources of income.

Paragraph 3

As a professional gamer, I earn money through various ways such as from <u>winning tournament prizes, advertising money from streaming my games on websites</u> such as Twitch or YouTube (plus online videos talking about the games) and even donations from fans. My dream would be for a big company to sponsor me, but that's a long way off. This industry is growing rapidly, and the potential for earning money as a professional gamer is increasing. However, it requires commitment, talent and hard work to succeed in this competitive field. And I'm 100% committed – I couldn't imagine doing anything else.

Answers | Part 5

✗	A	'He has yet to make money' means he does not earn already. The text contradicts this: *As a professional gamer, I **earn** money...*
✗	B	Being sponsored is something he hopes for in the future: *My dream would be for a big company to sponsor me, but that's a long way off.*
✗	C	He does not rely on his fans to pay: *even donations from fans* are one of his sources of income. The word 'even' suggests that it is not a regular or reliable source of come. These are donations, rather than payments.
✓	D	'several sources of income' – *winning tournament prizes, advertising money from streaming my games on websites...*

---

34. In line 20, what does 'my days are a balancing act' mean?

    A   The author feels the pressure to perform for his fans.

    | B | The author has to manage many things simultaneously. |

    C   The author has days where he has to do competitions and promotion.

    D   The author needs to manage gaming and another job.

Paragraph 4

Nowadays, <u>my days are a balancing act between practising, streaming my games to my audience, and responding to comments from my followers and taking breaks</u> to avoid getting too tired. When I get into my game setup in the morning, I fill out my schedule for the day – I might spend a few hours practising for the next competition, reviewing past games or taking part in online tournaments.

✗	A	No reference to his feeling pressure from fans (*followers*), although he does spend *some time responding to comments from my followers.*
✓	B	He does a lot of things at the same time ('simultaneously'): *my days are a balancing act between practising, streaming my games ... responding to comments from my followers ... taking breaks.*
✗	C	The writer does not say he **has** to do competitions. This would suggest pressure. He says: *my schedule for the day – I might spend a few hours practising for the next competition.* The word 'might' suggests it's a possible part of his schedule.
✗	D	There is no suggestion that the writer does another job.

B2 Reading | Cambridge Masterclass

35. In the fifth paragraph, the author talks about gaming and says that he

   A   doesn't enjoy it as much as he used to.

   B   thinks he will probably need to quit gaming soon.

   C   usually enjoys it but sometimes it's not so much fun.

   D   knows he has quite a heavy addiction to it.

Paragraph 5

Despite how much I love gaming, there are times when I do get bored of it. Some people get addicted to video games, and it can be hard for them to step away from the screen. But when I feel that way, I know it's time to quit for a while and focus on something else. The cycling helps with this, but I also like to read or do some drawing.

✗   A   There is no indication in the blog that the author enjoys it less than he did. He says: *Despite how much I love gaming...*

✗   B   The author admits that, if he thinks he may be getting addicted: *I know it's time to quit for a while and focus on something else.*

✓   C   *Despite how much I love gaming... I do get bored of it.*

✗   D   The author makes the point that **he** doesn't get addicted: *Some people get addicted to video games.*

---

36. Which games does the author say are his favourites?

   A   The games that made him fall in love with gaming.

   B   The competitive multi-player games.

   C   The games that are the most popular at the time.

   D   The games that can make him the most money.

Paragraph 6

The choice of which game to play can depend on various factors such as personal preference, skill level and the current popularity of a game. Some games can make professionals more money than others – financially, the big multi-player battle games are the ones to get into. As for my personal favourite, it's hard to choose just one. There are so many incredible games out there, each with their unique strengths and weaknesses. However, I have a particular love for League of Monsters and all the games that made me try competitive gaming.

Answers | Part 5

✓ **A** *...I have a particular love for League of Monsters and all the games that made me try competitive gaming* ('particular love' = favourites)

✗ **B** He says *financially, the big, multi-player battle games are the ones to get into...* but not that these games are his favourites.

✗ **C** He refers to *the current popularity of a game* (games that are the most popular at the time), but not that these are his favourites.

✗ **D** There is no reference to earning money in this part of the blog.

Part 5: Put it to the test 2 | Answers (pages 18–19)

31. What led to the author becoming a midwife?

   A She loved being around babies.
   B She wanted to help other people.
   C She worked as a doctor before specialising.
   D She felt inspired by what she experienced at nursing school.

Paragraph 2

Alhough I've always loved babies, I decided to go into this profession because <u>I have always had a passion for helping others</u>. After finishing high school, I considered going to medical college to become a doctor, but in the end I did a nursing degree. I then went on to specialise in midwifery, which I knew immediately <u>was the right decision</u>. It was the perfect fit for me because I wanted to work in a field where I could <u>make a difference in people's lives</u>, and being a midwife allows me to do just that.

✗ **A** The author says *I've always loved babies...* but her main motivation is helping people, especially new parents.

✓ **B** *...have always had a passion for helping others.*

✗ **C** She didn't work as a doctor... *I considered going to medical college to become a doctor...*

✗ **D** She does not mention *nursing school* or *inspiration*, but did *a nursing degree*.

Note: 'doctor' is a distractor. She didn't go to medical college.

81

32. In the third paragraph, the author explains that the best part of her job is

- A seeing a parent's reaction to their new baby.
- B the salary she is paid
- C the flexibility to work when she wants.
- D being there when the baby arrives.

Paragraph 3

It's not the best-paid job and my schedule depends on other people, <u>but</u> I wouldn't change it. <u>The most amazing part of my job is being present for the birth of a baby.</u>

- ✗ A There is no mention of parents' reaction to births.
- ✗ B *It's not the most well-paid job...* **but** *I wouldn't change it*
- ✗ C There is no flexibility. She says: *my schedule depends on other people...*
- ✓ D *The most amazing part of my job is being present for the birth of a baby.*

Note: The word 'but' shows that being well-paid is not important.

---

33. What does the author say about her relationships with her patients?

- A She enjoys helping and informing new mothers.
- B She usually only sees patients for their first child.
- C She often sees new parents lose confidence.
- D She is very involved in the weeks after the baby arrives.

Paragraph 5

Being a midwife, I love the relationships I build with my patients. It's not unusual for me to see the same women for several pregnancies, and it's always a joy to see how their families grow and change over time. Although I tend to be a bit hands-off after the birth, <u>I still love being able to provide education and support to new mothers</u>, and to see the <u>confidence</u> they gain as they become more comfortable in their roles as parents.

Answers | Part 5

✓	A	...*love being able to provide education and support to new mothers*...
✗	B	She sometimes sees the same mother several times: ...*not unusual for me to see the same women for several pregnancies*...
✗	C	This answer is the opposite of what she says: ...*see the confidence they gain*. To 'gain' **confidence** is the opposite of to 'lose' confidence.
✗	D	She is not very involved after the baby arrives: *Although I tend to be a bit hands-off after the birth*... ('hands-off' means the opposite of 'involved').

Note: 'confidence' is a distractor.

---

34. By attending a variety of births, the author has been

    A surprised that births often go more smoothly in a hospital setting.

    B interested to find out that births usually require hospital involvement.

    C surprised that births can be completely different for each person.

    D interested to learn that births are different if the mother is a very active person.

Paragraph 6

I've had the pleasure of attending a variety of births, from natural home births to hospital births with medical assistance. It's always a new experience <u>to see the different ways women choose to give birth</u>, and I've learned a lot from each experience. Last week alone I had one patient who was a professional athlete and continued running up until the day she gave birth, and another patient who came in to have one baby and left with twins!

✗	A	The author mentions hospital settings but does not suggest that births go more smoothly in hospital – ...*variety of births, from natural home births to hospital births*...
✗	B	The author mentions that hospital settings *include medical assistance*... but not that hospital births **require** this.
✓	C	*It's always a new experience to see the different ways women choose to give birth*. This suggests **surprise**.
✗	D	She refers to a mother who is very active (a professional athlete) but not that this makes births different.

35. In line 25, 'think on your feet' means

- **A** to know how to deal with delivery issues safely.
- **B** to carefully follow the birth plan.
- **C** to be able to move around while working.
- **D** to react as necessary at the time.

Paragraph 7

However, in this line of work it's important to be able to think on your feet because things can change quickly during labour and delivery. It's crucial to be able to adapt to new situations as they come up. In the past, I've had to cancel birth plans and make quick decisions based on the safety of both mother and baby.

✗ **A** Thinking about safety is important, but this is not 'think on your feet' means.

✗ **B** The author mentions *cancelling birth plans...* but this is not what 'think on your feet' means.

✗ **C** 'Thinking on your feet' does not involve walking or any physical movement.

✓ **D** ...crucial to be able to adapt to new situations...

36. In the final paragraph, what does the author say about her career?

- **A** She will be passionate about it for the remainder of her working life.
- **B** She thinks the hardest thing is hiding her emotions from patients.
- **C** She finds it difficult to give everything to her job, all of the time.
- **D** She feels that everyone would enjoy the job if they knew what it involved.

Paragraph 9

Even in those difficult moments, I know that I'm doing everything I can to give 100% to my patients. I realise that being a midwife is not for everyone, but for those who have a passion for it there's nothing else like it in the world. I feel incredibly lucky to be able to do what I do, and I know I will continue to find enjoyment in this career for as long as I do it. Despite how I feel, the job definitely has its challenges, like the emotions it produces in you and balancing work and personal life...

Answers | Part 5

✓ A   *...I know I will continue to find enjoyment in this career for as long as I do it.*

✗ B   She refers to her emotions but not that she hides them from patients.

✗ C   She says she gives everything: *I know that I'm doing everything I can to give 100% to my patients – Even in those difficult moments* – in other words: all of the time.

✗ D   She knows not everyone would enjoy her job: *I realise that being a midwife is not for everyone...*

B2 Reading | Cambridge Masterclass

Part 6: Practise I Answers   (pages 22–23)

Extract 1

The TV quiz programme 'Who Wants to Be a Millionaire?' is essentially a knowledge-based game show that tests the intelligence, quick thinking and bravery of its contestants. **This show consists of a series of multiple-choice questions of increasing difficulty, with a choice of four possible answers for each question.** Contestants must choose the correct option to continue in the game and eventually try to win the top prize.

| 1 | D |

'choice' = option

One of the show's most famous features is the system of lifelines*, which provide contestants with assistance when they encounter challenging questions. **The most well-known of these* is 'Phone-a-Friend', which lets contestants call a chosen individual for help.** The 'Ask the Audience' lifeline allows contestants to rely on the combined knowledge of the studio audience, and '50:50' removes two incorrect answers, leaving the contestant with a 50% chance of choosing the correct option. These lifelines add an element of strategy to the game, as contestants must decide when and how to use them effectively.

| 2 | C |

* The most well-known of these... 'these' = these lifelines

The success of 'Who Wants to Be a Millionaire?' is due not only to its engaging gameplay but also in the charm of its hosts. Throughout the show's history, there have been many different hosts, each bringing their own unique style and personality. From the popular original host, Chris Tarrant, who was presenter of the UK version for 15 years, to the current UK host Jeremy Clarkson, each host has left their mark on the show*. **Their humour** and ability to build excitement keep viewers on the edge of their seats, improving the overall experience of both TV and studio audiences.**

| 3 | A |

* ...mark on the show... = the missing sentence describes marks presenters leave.
** Their humour... = the humour of the presenters referred to in the text.

Sentence B does not fit any of the gaps. The subject matter could relate to missing sentence D, which refers to the level of difficulty of the questions. The word *these* does not refer back to anything earlier.

Answers | Part 6

Extract 2

In addition to its television success, the show has expanded into <u>other forms of media</u>. **It has inspired <u>board games and computer games</u>, allowing fans to experience the excitement of the competition themselves.** <u>These adaptations</u>* provide an interactive experience, in which players can test their knowledge and decision-making skills just like the show's contestants. The popularity of these games demonstrates the enduring appeal of 'Who Wants to Be a Millionaire?' beyond the television screen. Furthermore, the franchise's influence has even extended to the big screen with the world-famous film 'Slumdog Millionaire'.

| 1 | C |

> * *These adaptations* = ...board games and computer games...

Furthermore, the franchise's influence has even extended to the big screen with the world-famous film 'Slumdog Millionaire'. Directed by Danny Boyle, the movie tells the story of <u>Jamal Malik, a young boy</u> who appears on the Indian version of 'Who Wants to Be a Millionaire'. **The film explores the life experiences that help <u>the youngster</u> answer <u>the quiz questions</u>** correctly.

| 2 | D |

> The use of the definite article 'the' in '...**the** youngster...' refers back to the first mention of '...**a** young boy...' in the text.

According to well-known psychologist <u>Dr. Sarah Johnson</u>, 'Who Wants to Be a Millionaire?' connects with our human brains in a way that makes it fascinating for both contestants and viewers. **<u>She explains</u> that the way the show works brings together elements of knowledge-testing, decision-making under pressure and the appeal of a life-changing reward.** <u>This combination</u>* creates a powerful mixture of excitement and tension that causes the release of chemicals in the brain. The expectation of a potential million-pound prize stimulates...

| 3 | A |

> * *This combination...* = the missing sentence brings together elements of knowledge-testing, decision-making under pressure and the appeal of a life-changing reward.

Sentence B does not fit any of the gaps. The subject of the sentence 'She' is someone who wins the top prize, but the only person in the text who wins the top prize is the boy in the film 'Slumdog Millionaire'. The only 'she' referred to in the text is Dr Sarah Johnson, a psychologist, not a contestant in a show.

B2 Reading | Cambridge Masterclass

Part 6: Put it to the test 1 | Answers (pages 24–25)

The Covid-19 pandemic has had a huge impact on education worldwide, particularly in developing countries. **While some of these countries were able to adapt quickly to online learning and remote teaching, others were not so lucky**, leaving many students struggling to keep up with their studies. In this report, we will examine the impact of the pandemic on education in the developing world, with a focus on six specific countries.

| 37 | C |

Further reading of the text shows that the six specific countries are those that were 'not so lucky'.

At the beginning of the pandemic, many developing countries were forced to close schools and pause face-to-face learning. **This was a huge problem for a significant number of students who were already struggling to get by on limited resources.** Online education was not an option for many of these students due to a lack of internet access, computers, and other necessary equipment.

| 38 | G |

...close schools... = This was a huge problem ('This' refers back to school closures).

Similarly, in Pakistan, where many students rely on public schools, the pandemic put children's education at risk. According to a recent survey conducted by the National Education Association, 30% of Pakistani students did not attend online classes due to a lack of resources, while others struggled to keep up with the pace of online learning.

| 39 | A |

Nigeria is the subject of the previous paragraph. The missing sentence starts with 'Similarly'. The writer is comparing Pakistan with Nigeria. The text and the missing sentence both mention Pakistan.

However, despite these challenges, many developing countries have been working to make up for lost time and to find ways to help students catch up with their studies. In Bangladesh, for example, the government has provided free online education to students during the pandemic and has distributed radios and televisions to those who do not have internet access.

| 40 | E |

This paragraph compares Bangladesh favourably with Afghanistan. Bangladesh has managed to help children by providing resources not available in Afghanistan. The word 'However' introduces an idea that contrasts with what has gone before.

Answers | Part 6

In Myanmar, where the pandemic has put the education of millions of children at risk, the government has been working to provide all students with access to online education. **It has been working with international organisations to provide devices and internet access to students who lack these resources.**

The pronoun 'It' refers back to 'government' in the previous sentence.

Despite these efforts, there is still much work to be done to ensure that students in developing countries are not left behind due to the pandemic. **One major help would be for governments and organisations to take account of the unique challenges facing students in these countries and provide the necessary support to help them catch up with their studies.** They must also continue to explore alternative approaches to education and provide resources to help students get over the impact of the pandemic on their mental health and well-being.

If students are 'left behind', they need to 'catch up'.

Sentence D does not fit any of the gaps. Governments and other organisations are mentioned in the text but not NGOs (Non-governmental organisations). The word 'The' in sentence D would be referring back to a previous mention.

Part 6: Put it to the test 2 | Answers (pages 26–27)

The world of buying and selling sports shoes has become a crazy and highly profitable industry. **In recent years, it has brought in a new word to describe people involved in the industry.** 'Sneakerheads', as they are often called, are people who collect and trade rare or limited-edition sneakers, and who are willing to pay a lot of money for the most unique pairs. Here, we will explore the ins and outs of the sneaker market and highlight a successful seller who has made a name for himself in this highly competitive industry.

The pronoun 'it' in the missing sentence refers back to 'industry' in the text.
'word' in the missing sentence is named as 'Sneakerheads' in the text.

89

B2 Reading | Cambridge Masterclass

To start with, the sneaker market has become a global phenomenon, with buyers and sellers all over the world. **Many sneakerheads set up their own online stores or social media accounts to show their collections and attract potential buyers.** Some even figure out ways to create unofficial versions of highly rare sneakers in order to buy up stock at lower prices and sell on at a significant profit.

| 38 | F |

'buyers and sellers' in the text are referred to as 'sneakerheads' in the missing sentence.

'Some' refers to a number of the 'Many sneakerheads' mentioned in the missing sentence.

Sneakerheads are typically looking for rare or limited-edition sneakers, especially those with a unique design, history or connection to a well-known brand or artist. **They may also be interested in old or classic sneakers that have become highly popular and searched for over time.** Some examples of sneakers that sneakerheads might look out for include the Nike Air Jordan 1, Adidas Yeezy Boost and the Converse Chuck Taylor All-Star.

| 39 | A |

'They' in the missing sentence refers to 'Sneakerheads' in the first part of the text.

'also' in 'also be interested' in the missing sentence is in addition to 'rare or limited-edition sneakers' in the text.

In 2023, a pair of game-worn Nike Air Jordan sneakers sold for a record $2.2 million, making it the most expensive sneaker ever sold. **It is worth noting, however*, that most sneakerheads so not spend such high amounts on their collections, and there are many sneakers available at lower prices**** for those who are interested in the hobby.

| 40 | E |

'such high amounts' in the missing sentence refers to '$2.2 million' in the text.

* 'however' in the missing sentence points out contrasting information.

** 'at lower prices' means lower than the high prices mentioned previously.

One example of a successful sneaker trader is Benjamin Kickz, who is known as the 'Sneaker Don'. He started his business at the young age of 13 by buying and selling shoes online. He quickly made connections in the industry and started shopping around for rare and exclusive sneakers He used to jump into queues, paying huge amounts of money to get his hands on limited-edition pairs. **As his reputation grew, he started to make a name for himself among the celebrity crowd, with clients such as Drake, DJ Khaled and Chris Brown.** Benjamin Kickz later expanded into clothing and jewellery as well.

| 41 | C |

90

Answers | Part 6

'Benjamin Kickz' is described as 'a successful sneaker trader' in the text, who manages to 'make a name for himself' in the missing sentence.

'his reputation' in the missing sentence refers to 'Benjamin Kickz' earlier and later in the text, and all the uses of the pronoun 'he'.

The sneaker industry is highly competitive and can be challenging, unless you have a reputation like Benjamin. **Successful sellers like him² know that they must bear in mind the latest trends and keep an eye on the market to stay ahead.** A well-timed phone call or message to their network of contacts can keep them informed and maintain their position as a top seller.

| 42 | G |

Successful sellers must keep an eye on the market to maintain their position as a top seller because the sneaker market is highly competitive.

Successful sellers like him in the missing sentence refers to Benjamin (Kickz) in the text.

Sentence B does not fit any of the gaps. The initial word it in Sentence B does not relate to anything in any of the sentences preceding any of the gaps. The paragraph that includes Gap 38 mentions social media and the paragraph that contains Gap 41 mentions a successful sneakerhead, but these are distractors as there are no specific language links.

B2 Reading | Cambridge Masterclass

Part 7: Practise 1 | Answers   (pages 30–31)

---

1. Which person worked with teenagers?

   Text B: ...*camp was designed for curious minds* **between the ages of 12 and 15**... | 1 | B |

2. Which person worked with children with scientific interests?

   Text B: ...*who were enthusiastic about* **science, technology, engineering**... | 2 | B |

3. Which person mentions a weekly competition?

   Text A: ...*the sports* **tournament** *held at the end of* **each week**. | 3 | A |
   ('tournament' = competition)

4. Which person tried to develop children's ability to solve problems?

   Text B: ...*encouraged critical thinking and* **problem-solving skills**... | 4 | B |

5. Which person mentions that children's relatives saw what they had done?

   Text B: ...*demonstrated their individual projects to other children and* **their parents**. | 5 | B |

6. Which person encouraged children to work together in groups?

   Text A: ...*working* **as a team**. | 6 | A |

Part 7: Practise 2 | Answers   (pages 32–33)

---

1. Which person describes how the children felt proud of what they achieved?

   Text B: *You could see the sense of* **achievement and pride** *that showed*... | 1 | B |

2. Which person mentions that children made something unusual for people to wear?

   Text B: ...*creating* **unique jewellery**... | 1 | B |

3. Which person describes a camp situated in a wooded area?

   Text A: ...*located in the middle of a picturesque* **forest, surrounded by tall trees**... | 3 | A |

4. Which person describes activities that encouraged children to work together?

   Text B: ...*projects that required* **cooperation and the children to work in teams**. | 4 | B |

92

5. Which person describes how the children became more confident due to their experience?

Text B: ...*develop their communication skills and increase their confidence*.

| 5 | B |

6. Which person mentions that their group camped at night?

Text A: ...*overnight camping trip. We set up tents...*

| 6 | A |

Part 7: Put it to the test 1 | Answers   (pages 34–35)

43. Which person mentions that they work somewhere that sells used items at a discount?

Text B: ...*charity shop worker ... variety of unwanted items that come into the shop that can now be sold for much less...*

| 43 | B |

44. Which person believes that helping those who have been affected by social or political violence is very satisfying?

Text C: *Syria...conflict in the country ... displaced by the conflict ... such difficult circumstances.*

| 44 | C |

45. Which person describes how volunteering allows them to meet people from different backgrounds?

Text A: *people from all walks of life* = people with different types of jobs and from different levels of society.

| 45 | A |

46. Which person finds that volunteering is a great way to spend time now that they've finished work?

Text B: *It's a great way to keep busy now that I'm retired.*
(to be 'retired' = to have finished working, usually on reaching a certain age)

| 46 | B |

47. Which person states that their listening skills are crucial for their volunteering work?

Text D: *The ability to listen patiently is key ... By being sympathetic and listening, we can help make a difference in someone's life...*
('key' and 'crucial' = very important)

| 47 | D |

48. Which person says that they're always curious about the range of things that end up at their charity shop?

Text B: *It's always interesting to see the variety of items that come into the shop...*

| 48 | B |

49. Which person suggests that the speed of modern life can make people feel alone?

Text D: ...*the world being so fast-moving* and stressful, it's easy for *people to feel lonely*...

| 49 | D |

50. Which person thinks that they have learned to appreciate everything they have because of their volunteer work?

Text C: ...(the work) reminds me *to be grateful* for the simple things *I have in my life*.
(In this context, 'to be grateful for' = to appreciate)

| 50 | C |

51. Which person explains that they will return to their studies after their volunteer work?

Text C: *Taking a year out from university ... and take part in volunteer work*.
(It is sometimes called a gap year = when students leave the place of study for a time, then go back after the 'gap'.)

| 51 | C |

52. Which person says that it's important not to judge those that need help?

Text A: *It's essential to treat everyone with kindness and respect whatever their circumstances*.

| 52 | A |

Part 7: Put it to the test 2 | Answers   (pages 36–37)

43. Which person explains that cats have bad attitudes?

Text C: *For me, cats are so arrogant ... a cat would eat you if they could. ...judging your every move*.

| 43 | C |

44. Which person thinks that it's nice when a cat doesn't demand affection?

Text A: *I respect cats for their independence. ...when they're not in the mood for socialising*, but that's just part of their charm.

| 44 | A |

45. Which person mentions that they have several pets?

Text B: *I have a pack of dogs*...

| 45 | B |

46. Which person believes that despite the attention of strangers, their pets' appearance isn't important?

Text B: *It's enjoyable for me to see how nice they look and how much attention they get from the public. But, at the end of the day, it's not about how my dogs look*...

| 46 | B |

Watch out for distractors — information that may lead to choosing a wrong answer!

Answers | Part 7

47. Which person suggests that looking after a dog would take up more time than a cat?

Text C: Secondly, let's talk about **energy levels**. Dogs will **play until they get tired**, and then **they'll still want to go for a walk**.

| 47 | C |

48. Which person states that cats demand much less attention than dogs?

Text A: ...dogs can be so needy (whereas cats) don't need constant attention or approval...

| 48 | A |

49. Which person sounds as though they're trying to justify the idea of getting a pet?

Text D: I've been **unsure about having a pet, but if I were to get one**, I think I would go for a cat. I don't have any pets at the moment... the more I think about it...

| 49 | D |

50. Which person finds that training a pet is essential to avoid trouble?

Text A: To me, **dogs can do more harm than good**, especially **if they're not taught properly**.

| 50 | A |

51. Which person believes that cats are less energetic than dogs?

Text C: ...let's talk about **energy levels**. Good luck trying to get a cat to fetch something or go for a run. Dogs will play until they get tired ... They'll (cats) **sit on the arm of the sofa**...

| 51 | C |

52. Which person explains that their pets are a good way of staying healthy?

Text B: ...they're (dogs) the perfect excuse for a **good walk**. My **dogs keep me fit and active**...

| 52 | B |

Practise test 1 | Answers

(pages 42–47)

Part 5		Key words from the questions	Clues from the text
31	C	They have a variety of life experiences	from many different backgrounds
32	A	She had heard other travellers' accounts of making the journey	The stories of self-discovery / had fascinated her for years
33	D	Making meaningful contact with so many different people.	Maria had serious conversations with these diverse individuals
34	B	Everything she has to think about during her home life.	disconnect from the noise of daily life and focus on my inner thoughts
35	C	make more contact with people in the areas the route went through.	more time interacting with the locals and immersing myself in the culture of the regions I passed through.
36	B	the walk had improved her physical condition	I had not considered how much my general fitness would benefit

Part 6		Key words from the questions	Clues from the text
37	B	It has been a battleground	chess has been more than simply a game
38	C	this new interest / new technology and the rise of media platforms.	This development
39	E	These platforms have created a global	Platforms like chess.com / players and fans from around the world
40	G	powerful chess engines like Stockfish	revolutionising the way players study and prepare for games / These AI-powered tools
41	A	chess has found its way onto the small screen	the influence of television programmes / The Netflix mini-series
42	F	This interactive feature	now regularly livestream their matches, providing useful commentary and communicating with viewers / The popularity of chess streamers

Part 7		Key words from the questions	Clues from the text
43	D	have to play at times they would rather spend with friends and family	working on weekends and holidays, giving up personal time with my loved ones
44	A	finds it difficult to make enough money	trying to earn a living from my art has been incredibly challenging
45	C	enjoys playing with other musicians, but finds it limiting	I really want to explore my own musical ideas / it's a wonderful experience
46	B	receives some of their income from audience members	the tips from enthusiastic tourists can be generous
47	D	on celebratory occasions	wedding singer / be a part of people's special day
48	A	feels discouraged by the challenges	It's depressing / the constant uncertainty … I'm always experiencing self-doubt
49	B	pattern of work allows them time to get better at playing music	regular schedule that allows me to focus on my craft and continue improving my skills
50	A	difficult to find enough opportunities to play	There are few opportunities for gigs
51	C	no choice about what and how they play	means sticking to strict musical interpretations and following a conductor's lead
52	D	a range of very different venues	my work exciting. From small garden ceremonies to receptions in massive houses or hotels,

Practise test 2 | Answers

(pages 50–55)

Part 5		Key words from the questions	Clues from the text
31	C	affects the length of time when pollen levels are high	changing climate, which leads to longer pollen seasons
32	A	bodies respond more strongly than they should	the body's natural defence to disease, over-reacts to harmless things
33	B	their eyes react more than normal to light	can become super sensitive to light.
34	D	make their eyes and nose less painful	nasal sprays or eye drops to reduce inflammation
35	B	condition is not improved by medicines that can be bought easily	doesn't get better with over-the-counter treatments, it's a good idea to see a doctor
36	A	Some forecasts broadcast information about pollen levels	pollen levels each day / This information is sometimes included in weather forecasts

Part 6		Key words from the questions	Clues from the text
37	D	to challenge himself by running his first marathon	got him started in Extreme Marathon running / The thrill of completing that race started a desire within me
38	G	more than just physical challenges; they're a journey of self-discovery	drives him to participate in those incredibly challenging races / I believe that by pushing myself to the edge
39	A	one of the most memorable races he had participated in was the 'Desert Storm Ultra'	an example of an extreme marathon that left a lasting impression on him / This was held in the deserts of Namibia
40	F	complete determination to overcome these dangers fuelled my spirit	dehydration became a real threat / Crossing the finish line was an experience I'll remember forever.
41	B	how he stayed motivated during the long and demanding hours	mental strength required for such races must be huge / Mental strength is undoubtedly crucial.

Answers | Practice test 2

| 42 | E | I research the course, understand the potential dangers involved | Safety is the most important thing / I also equip myself with the correct gear |

Part 7		Key words from the questions	Clues from the text
43	B	learn a lot about digital technology in a short time	their learning curve for digital tools has been steeper
44	C	time when the economy was unpredictable	We grew up during a time of economic instability
45	A	educated in a rather old-fashioned way	We relied on traditional teaching methods
46	D	understand how shoppers think and act	understanding of online platforms and consumer behaviour
47	B	appreciates having grown up in a technologically advanced world	am grateful for the technological developments that have shaped our lives
48	A	capable of doing many things simultaneously	displaying remarkable multi-tasking abilities
49	B	able to make links between digital technology and older ways of working	bridge the gap between traditional methods and digital innovation
50	C	understands the need to plan for the future?	keen understanding of risk management, long-term planning
51	D	their generation is both imaginative and technically capable makes them different	Our ability to use creativity with technology equally well sets us apart
52	D	Generation X has had to get used to the idea that business can be done digitally	Generation X has had to adapt to the rise of digital marketing

Practise test 3 | Answers (pages 58–63)

Part 5		Key words from the questions	Clues from the text
31	B	the best location and atmosphere	a suitable environment
32	D	Plants find the process of being moved disturbing	plants feel shock when they are transplanted
33	A	add organic matter to the soil	enriching it with compost – the decaying remains of other plants, or manure
34	C	produce tomatoes for a longer period of time	extension of the tomato-growing season
35	B	choose plants that produce small tomatoes	Select plants that will not grow large fruits
36	A	helps the plants to produce a better crop of tomatoes	to help redirect energy towards fruit production

Part 6		Key words from the questions	Clues from the text
37	F	sound of our feathered friends	a familiar song fills the air,
38	B	heart of nature; an opportunity to witness the beauty of the avian world	is an activity that is bigger than just observation / For me, the attraction lies in the sense of connection it creates between humanity and the natural world.
39	A	In a world with the constant background noise of technology	bird watching apart is the deep sense of calm it creates / The simple act of walking through nature
40	C	Every bird has unique characteristics	colourful feathers of the kingfisher to the majestic flight of birds of prey
41	D	unexpected encounters	watching gives us is the element of surprise / The excitement of spotting

42	G	It requires no special skills or extensive knowledge	an activity that can be enjoyed by all / All that is needed is an open heart and a sense of curiosity

Part 7		Key words from the questions	Clues from the text
43	C	more interested in using words than with telling the story well	showing off his vocabulary rather than adding to the story
44	B	found the pace of the novel was inconsistent	development of the story moved too fast at times and too slowly at others
45	D	writer makes readers think about life today	thought-provoking representation of contemporary
46	A	they discussed the ideas in it with people they knew	to have conversations about morality and justice with friends and members of my family
47	C	the story of the novel too pessimistic	be unnecessarily dark and without hope
48	A	found the novel interesting because of some surprising things that happened	some unexpected events that certainly kept me interested
49	B	liked the basic idea of the novel but found how it was written as a novel disappointing?	the concept of the story seemed interesting, the way in which it was turned into a novel was poor
50	B	didn't care about what happened to the characters	uninterested in the fate of the characters
51	D	praises how the writer describes the characters complete with their faults	characters are excellently described, each with their own strengths and weaknesses
52	A	characters in the novel simple to connect with	making them easy to relate to

Practise test 4 | Answers

Part 5		Key words from the questions	Clues from the text
31	C	make the lives of the people who live in cities better	improving the quality of life for the residents
32	A	reach the facilities they need easily and quickly	neighbourhoods that can meet most of people's daily needs within a 15-minute walk or bike ride from their homes
33	D	impact communities have on the natural environment	Green planning incorporates sustainable design principles / efficient waste-management / preservation of green spaces.
34	B	do not allow water to run away	impermeable materials, such as concrete and asphalt 34 which restrict natural water drainage
35	C	residents of cities should be involved in planning	crucial to get residents to take part in the planning process
36	A	examples of positive urban planning	Paris has made significant progress in transforming itself into a 15-minute city / Copenhagen, known for its commitment to cycling infrastructure / Singapore has also emerged as a leader in porous-city design

Part 6		Key words from the questions	Clues from the text
37	B	However, it faced opposition	the sport gained popularity among women in England. / It wasn't until the mid-20th century
38	G	This event marked a turning point	the first Women's World Cup was held in China / The tournament's success
39	D	Organisations have been established to promote the sport among girls	increase in participation from young players / This has resulted in a larger pool
40	F	The success of players like Mia Hamm and Ada Hegerberg has broken through 'glass ceilings' / strong female role models.	The visibility of female footballers has been crucial / Their achievements on the field

Answers | Practice test 4

41	C	It has provided... / ... challenging assumptions about gender and sports	Women's football has played a significant role in promoting gender equality in sports / The increased visibility ... has contributed to broader conversations about equal pay
42	A	Gender pay gaps, inequalities / areas that require attention	there are still challenges to overcome / However, the progress made so far

Part 7		Key words from the questions	Clues from the text
43	D	responsible for the whole life	take responsibility for the entire life-cycle of their products
44	B	recycling companies may lose business	leads to decreased demand for recycled goods
45	C	lists of materials that could replace plastic packaging	alternatives such as cloth bags, goods sold in carboard packages and refillable water bottles
46	A	mixture of recyclable and unrecyclable goods may end up being buried in the ground?	recycling facilities have to send contaminated materials to waste landfill sites
47	C	consumers should find out for themselves the recycling policies	inform themselves about local recycling services and guidelines
48	B	different regions may have different recycling policies	local recycling programmes that differ widely from area to area
49	A	list of materials that some consumers put in recycling bins	plastic bags, polystyrene foam and certain plastics that may or may not be accepted by recycling
50	C	no longer depend on products that can only be used once	reduce the extent to which they rely on single-use items
51	D	state clearly whether their products can be recycled	Manufacturers can play a vital role ... by clearly labelling products to inform consumers about recyclability
52	D	new laws could be brought in to improve the situation	governments can introduce legislation

www.ingramcontent.com/pod-product-compliance
Lightning Source LLC
Chambersburg PA
CBHW051348110526
44591CB00025B/2942